ACKNOWLEDGMENTS

A special thanks to all those who have contributed to my knowledge
and brought the book together. Mum & Dad, for teaching
and encouraging me to appreciate boutique and craft alcohol
instead of abusing it. My sister Charlie, who introduced me to
the hospitality industry. Sam & Josh, who taught me so much
foundational knowledge about the world of mixology and alcohol.
Fleur, for designing and creating the book and brand. Madison,
for writing and editing the text. And of course, to Mike, for
encouraging me to create the book and bringing it all alive!

Authors: George Grbich and Madison Fisher
Contributor: Tash McGill
Design: Fleur Curac
Photography: Mike Timmer
Website: nzginguide.com
Instagram: @nzginguide
Facebook: Guide to New Zealand Gin

PUBLISHED BY

People Media Group
Newmarket, Auckland
peoplemediagroup.co.nz

CONTENTS

5 **The Team**
7 **Styles of Gin**
8 **Classic Botanicals**
9 **New Zealand Native Botanicals**

10 **CLASSIC GIN**
12 1919 Classic
13 Sir Winston Classic
14 batch10 New Zealand Dry Gin
15 Black Collar Gin
16 Black Robin Rare Gin
17 Broken Heart Angel's Share Gin
18 Broken Heart Gin
19 Broken Heart Queenstown Edition
20 The Source Gin
21 Old Jones London Dry Gin
22 Curiosity Gin - Curious Dry
23 Dancing Sands Dry Gin
24 Denzien Our Coast
25 Denzien Te Aro Dry
26 Good George Day Off Gin
27 Humdinger Citrus Gin
28 Humdinger Dry Gin
29 Reikorangi Dry Gin
30 Juno Extra Fine
31 Championz Gin
32 Delightful Dry Gin
33 Laughing Club Gin
34 Lighthouse Gin Original

35 No8 Dunners Dry Gin
36 Papaka Road Gin
37 Pink & White - White Dry
38 Reid + Reid Native Gin
39 Reid + Reid Rev. Dawson's Gin
40 Rifters Original Dry Gin
41 Roots Marlborough Dry Gin
42 The Valley Gin
43 Lovers Leap Gin
44 Scapegrace Classic
45 Solace Dry Gin
46 Twelfth Hour Dry Gin
47 The Vicar's Son Gin - Classic London Dry
48 Victor Gin Original
49 Waiheke Distilling Co. London Dry Gin
50 Waiheke Distilling Co. Spirit of Waiheke
51 Waitoki Gin

52 **CONTEMPORARY**
54 Ariki Ultra Premium Gin
55 Awildian Coromandel Dry
56 Awildian Coromandel Dry - Blue Edition
57 The Bond Store Kawakawa Gin
58 Bureaucrats: The Bureaucrat
59 Bureaucrats: The Doyenne
60 Curiosity Gin - Recipe #23

61 Denzien Smoke & Embers

62 Dr Beak Garden Gin

63 Dr Beak Premium Gin

64 Eliza's Claim Dry Gin

65 Eliza's Claim Gold Gin

66 Exhibit A No.580

67 1564 Venus & Adonis

68 The Artist

69 The Novelist

70 The Poet

71 The Vintner

72 Parma Violet

73 Signature Citrus

74 Albertine Gin

75 East Block 200 Gin

76 Wakame Seaweed Dry Gin

77 Island Gin Original

78 Greenstone Gin

79 Tini Remana Gin

80 Lady H Gin

81 Little Biddy Gin - Classic

82 Little Biddy Gin - Gold Label

83 Little Biddy Gin - Black Label

84 Mt. Fyffe Shearwater Gin

85 Mt. Fyffe Woolshed Gin

86 Adorn Beauty Gin

87 Hemp Gin

88 Meow Lucky Gin

89 New Zealand Dry Gin

90 NZ Native Gin - The Proof

91 Verdigris NZ Dry Gin

92 No8 Hibiscus Gin

93 No8 Horopito Fire Gin

94 Rifters Quartz Gin

95 1743 Riot

96 1920 Rose

97 Scapegrace Black

98 STORM Black Wolf Gin

99 Strange Nature Gin

100 Takapuna Butterfly Pea Flower

101 Carbon6 Black Gin

102 Victor Gin Kaffir Lime

103 Wild Diamond Black Gin

104 Wild Diamond Rare Dry Gin

106 **NAVY STRENGTH**

108 Broken Heart Navy Gin

109 Nine Fathoms Canterbury Gin

110 Island Gin Navy Strength

111 Lighthouse Hawthorn Edition

112 Old Navy - Navy Strength Gin

113 Roots Norwester Navy Strength Dry Gin

114 Scapegrace Gold

116 **PINK**

118 1919 Pink Gin

119 batch10 Pink Gin

120 Concept Distilling Pink Gin

121 Pink & White - Pink Dry

122 **FLAVOURED**

124 1919 Pinapple Bits Gin

125 Blush Boysenberry Gin

126 Blush Rhubarb Gin

127 Blush Hot Toddy Gin

128 Blush Summer Citrus Gin

129 Broken Heart Pinot Noir Gin

130 Broken Heart Quince Gin

131 Broken Heart Rhubarb Gin

132 Bureaucrats: Black Doris Plum

133 Concept Distilling Blood Orange Gin

134 Concept Distilling Blueberry Gin

135 Curiosity Gin - Ruby

136 Curiosity Gin - Pinot Barrel Sloe

137 Dancing Sands Sauvignon Blanc Gin

138 Dancing Sands Sun-Kissed Gin

139 Good George Day Off Doris Plum Gin

140 Good George Day Off Feijoa Gin

141 Damson Plum & Blackberry Gin Liqueur

142 Reikorangi Rhubarb & Raspberry Gin

143 Lavender Infused Gin

144 Saffron Infused Gin

145 Rose & Twig Blood Orange Gin

146 Rose & Twig Blueberry Gin

147 Rose & Twig Pomegranate Gin

148 Solace Raspbery & Cranberry Gin

149 Takapuna Berry Pink Gin

150 Takapuna Cheese Cake Gin

151 Takapuna Manuka Honey Gin

152 Takapuna Zesty Citrus Gin

153 Victor Gin Blanc de Blanc

154 Ruby Red Gin

155 Sheep Milk & Honey Gin

156 Wild Diamond Feijoa Gin

157 Wild Diamond Vanilla Gin

158 **AGED**

160 Awildian Coromandel Manuka Gin

161 Broken Heart Barrel Aged Gin

162 Curiosity Gin - Negroni Special

163 The Pioneer

164 Black Barn Syrah Barrel Aged Gin

165 Little Biddy Gin - Cask Aged

166 Reid + Reid Barrel Aged Gin

168 **ALCOHOL FREE SPIRIT**

170 Ecology & Co. Asian Spice

171 Ecology & Co. London Dry

172 **FEVER-TREE**

173 A Short History on Tonic

174 How to Create the Perfect Gin & Tonic

176 Tonics

178 Gingers

179 Sodas

181 **DISTILLERY DIRECTORY**

THE TEAM

GEORGE GRBICH - TASTER & AUTHOR

George is a spirits writer with 7 years of experience working in the Auckland hospitality industry. A passionate gin advocate whose love for spirits sprung from his father's love for a good gin and tonic. He is deeply intrigued by the variety of styles and techniques being used in the modern world of gin and is a strong supporter of the growing New Zealand spirits scene. As well as being an associate member of Distilled Spirits Aotearoa, he has also recently obtained his WSET Spirits Level 2 qualification.

TASH MCGILL - TASTER & CONTRIBUTOR

Tash is an international spirits writer, judge, and educator. She works as a consultant and advocate in the spirits and hospitality industry to see growth, sustainability, and health. Tash is also the host of More Good Booze, co-founder of The Feed, is currently studying for her Council of Whisky Masters certification, is Chair of the New Zealand Whisky Council and has obtained her WSET Spirits Level 2 qualification.

CLAIRE FILER - TASTER

Claire is an established advocate and influencer of New Zealand's spirits industry, and has been on judging panels for the NZ Spirits Awards and The Junipers Gin Awards. She is well known for her international spirits blogs High Ginx and Ginesthesia, about discovering the world of spirits through distillery visits and workshops across the world. Claire is also an associate member of Distilled Spirits Aotearoa and has obtained her WSET Spirits Level 2 qualification.

STEVE BENNET - TASTER

Steve Bennett, Master of Wine, has more than 30 years of experience working in the retail, importation, distribution, production, and educational sectors of the liquor industry. In 1994 he became the youngest ever of only 450 people to have passed the Master of Wine Examination. Steve has educated both consumers and liquor industry professionals in NZ, Australia, the US, UK, and Europe. As well as a strong professional interest in wine, Steve has a personal passion for beer and gin which he has tasted widely during his international travels.

We have condensed the **145** NZ Gins into **7** Categories

Classic – London dry and modern dry style gins

Contemporary – Contemporary dry and contemporary modern style gins

Navy Strength – Navy strength gins

Pink – Pink gins

Flavoured – Flavoured gins, sloe gins and gin liqueurs

Aged – Aged and barrel aged gins

Alcohol Free – Alcohol free spirits

Our tasters have selected a top pick in each category. Look out for this badge.

Our tasters have selected a range of highly commended gins from each section.

Our 2020 tasters selected a top pick from each category

STYLES OF GIN

London Dry: All botanical flavour must be imparted through distillation only. The addition of sweetener or sugar is prohibited. This classic style of gin is juniper dominant but also packed with citrus and uses classic botanicals such as coriander seed, angelica root, citrus peel and orris root are considered synonymous with the style.

Modern Dry: Juniper dominant and containing classical botanicals, a Modern Dry style will include modern and local botanicals to enhance its flavour and profile.

Contemporary Dry: Still juniper forward, unsweetened gins that may draw on modern botanicals as well.

Contemporary Modern: These are gins that still include juniper in the botanical profile but are not juniper forward relying on other modern botanicals to create unique flavour profiles.

Navy: The baseline for Navy Strength gin was traditionally the same style as London Dry but proofed at the higher ABV of 54.5% and above. Can be made in a Classic or Contemporary style.

Pink: A classic London Dry or Modern Dry gin that has natural pink colouring due to the redistillation of berries, red fruits or pink botanicals.

Flavoured: Made using compound methods or vacuum distillation to infuse or macerate flavour into gin.

Sloe Gin: A gin-based liqueur sweetened with sugar and flavoured by infusing sloe berries

Gin Liqueur: A gin liqueur may be infused or macerated with additional flavours, including the addition of sugar and typically bottled at a lower abv.

Aged Gin: An aged gin refers to any gin that has been finished for any period of time with additional ingredients or influence, including the addition of staves or woodchip in tank or keg prior to bottling. The use of wood components produces an aged effect and wood influence on the gin.

Barrel/Cask Aged Gin: Matured in barrel or cask for ant period of time.

Alcohol-Free Spirit: Distilled without the presence of alcohol resulting in a an alcohol-free distilled spirit.

CLASSIC BOTANICALS

JUNIPER

In ancient times, juniper was used as a spice and for medicinal purposes. It's dominantly pine-flavored and is responsible for the resinous, green notes often associated with gin.

CORIANDER

Coriander is the dried seed of the green plant and has a complex taste that is warm spice, slightly citrus and earthy or nutty when crushed.

ANGELICA

A common botanical used mostly as the root for its earthy, bitter complexity.

LEMON & ORANGE

Primarily used for its peel and pith to produce zesty, sweet and bitter citrus notes. As with lemon, orange peels are the most common part of the fruit used in gin production — and dried orange peel in particular. Depending on the type of orange used, the oils in the skin can provide bitter citrus or sweet and gentle notes.

ORRIS ROOT

Orris root has a floral and sweet aroma that's common in perfume as well as gin. It also adds an earthy and woody flavour.

CARDAMOM

Green cardamom pods are most often used in gin. They have a somewhat numbing and medicinal taste and, are highly aromatic. Black cardamom is also occasionally used.

LIQUORICE

Liqurice root is sweet and similar to anise. Liquorice is used for its sweetness and texture.

CASSIA BARK

Cassia bark strongly resembles the spicy hot bite of cinnamon but is just a little sweeter with a liquorice-like flavour.

CINNAMON

Cinnamon bark adds fiery and spicy notes to balance the sweet, woody, earthy and herbal notes of other classic botanicals.

NEW ZEALAND BOTANICALS

HOROPITO
For a peppery, citrus bite.

MANUKA
For woody sweetness and
light floral notes.

KAWAKAWA
For floral and spice notes, either
the berry or the leaf can be used.

KAHIKATEA
For slightly sweet, resinous notes.

TARATA
For lemon and citrus tones.

TOATOA
For tannic qualities and bitterness.

VICTOR GIN
V
WORLD SPIRITS COMPETITION
DOUBLE GOLD
NEW ZEALAND
1919
DISTILLING
GIN
Est. 2017
HAND-CRAFTED
SMALL BATCH
700ml
NEW ZEALAND MADE, DISTILLED & BOTTLED
ALC/VOL 41%
82 PROOF
JUNO
EXTRA FINE
GIN
700ml 40.0% Alc/Vol.
DENZIEN
URBAN DISTILLERY
SMALL GIN BATCH
OF NEW ZEALAND
700ml
TE ARO DRY
UNASHAMEDLY URBAN GIN
HAND CRAFTED IN WELLINGTON

CLASSIC

LONDON DRY

All botanical flavour must be imparted through distillation only. The addition of sweetener or sugar is prohibited. This classic style of gin is juniper dominant but also packed with citrus and uses classic botanicals such as coriander seed, angelica root, citrus peel and orris root are considered synonymous with the style.

MODERN DRY

Juniper dominant and containing classical botanicals, a Modern Dry style will include modern and local botanicals to enhance its flavour and profile.

1919 Classic

41% ABV

A modern dry style gin, 1919 Classic Gin celebrates old world charm with botanicals like juniper, angelica root, and cinnamon in combination with Otago cherries, manuka honey, and organic lemons and oranges.

DISTILLERY:
1919 Distilling, Auckland

BOTANICALS:
Juniper, Coriander Seed, Green Cardamom, Lemon Peel, Orange Peel, Angelica Root, Cherry, Manuka Honey & Cinnamon

---

TASTING NOTES:
Dry and tart citrus on the nose. Juniper is balanced with sweet, tart cherry, earthy coriander and citrus peel on the palate leading to a pleasing dry finish.

SERVING SUGGESTION:
Enjoy with Fever-Tree Premium Indian Tonic Water and a slice of lemon.

AWARDS:
NZ Artisan Awards — Alcohol Category Winner 2019, Australian Gin Awards — Silver 2019, NZ Spirits Awards - Silver 2020, Bronze 2021, and SIP Awards — Bronze 2020

Sir Winston Classic

40% ABV

A modern dry style gin, Sir Winston Classic is themed around its namesake and includes Churchill's favourite tea, Lapsang, among its botanicals.

DISTILLERY:
1919 Distilling, Auckland

BOTANICALS:
Juniper, Coriander Seed, Lapsang Tea, Cinnamon, Orris Root, Licorice Root, Lemon Peel & Orange Peel

TASTING NOTES:
Citrus and gentle smoke on the nose, delicate but well-rounded on the palate with coriander and black tea earthiness, marmalade tart and a dry, subtle smoky finish.

SERVING SUGGESTION:
Enjoy with Fever-Tree Premium Indian Tonic Water and a slice of lemon.

AWARDS:
NZ Spirits Awards - Gold 2021

batch10 New Zealand Gin

37% ABV

A classic style gin with a New Zealand twist, batch10 New Zealand Gin is smooth and crisp with a distinct hint of citrus that honours the orchards of the nearby Omaha and Matakana areas.

DISTILLERY:
batch10 Spirits, Puhoi

BOTANICALS:
Juniper, Coriander Seed, Cassia Bark, Angelica Root, Nutmeg, Citrus Peel, Tangerine, Orris Root, Star Anise, Anise, Lemon, Orange & Cardamom

---

TASTING NOTES:
Soft, subtle spice and coriander on the nose. Mouthfeel is also soft with juniper, lemon peel and baking spice for a very mild finish.

SERVING SUGGESTION:
Enjoy with Fever-Tree Premium Indian Tonic Water and a slice of lemon.

Black Collar Gin

42% ABV

A modern dry style gin, Black Collar Gin is made traditionally by macerating their botanicals overnight before distillation with no vapour infusion, water baths, essences, or artificial flavourings.

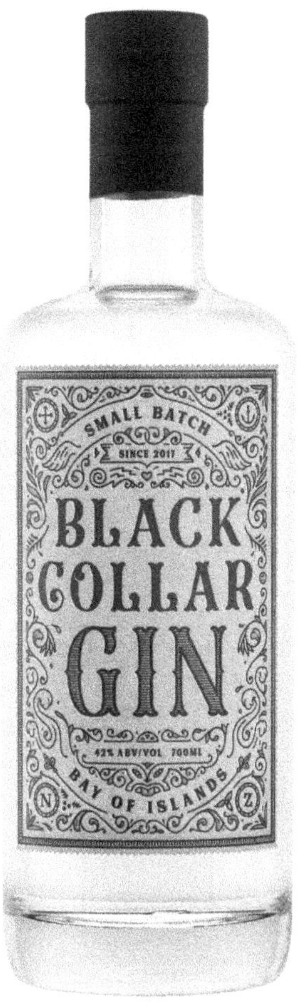

DISTILLERY:
Black Collar Distillery, Kerikeri

BOTANICALS:
Juniper, Coriander Seed, Liquorice Root, Marshmallow & Others

---

TASTING NOTES:
Damp, earthy nose with strong liquorice and nutty spice on the palate. Short, round finish.

SERVING SUGGESTION:
Enjoy with Fever-Tree Mediterranean Tonic Water and a slice of grapefruit.

AWARDS:
IWSC UK – Bronze Medal 2019

Black Robin Rare Gin

43% ABV

A modern dry style gin, Black Robin Rare Gin is five times distilled with a unique blend of botanicals, including some native to New Zealand to honour the Black Robin's heritage. The bottle's Black Robin artwork was originally hand-painted by renowned NZ artist Andrew Barns-Graham.

DISTILLERY:

Distillerie Deinlein, Te Puna

BOTANICALS:

Juniper, Chervil, Watercress, Parsley, Mint, Liquorice Root, Star Anise, Horopito, Candied Lime Zest, Candied Lemon Zest & Lemongrass

---

TASTING NOTES:

Candied citrus zest and forest floor on the nose, peppery horopito and sweet lemon on the palate with an aniseed dry finish.

SERVING SUGGESTION:

Enjoy with Fever-Tree Mediterranean Tonic Water and a slice of lime.

AWARDS:

San Francisco World Spirits Competition – Silver Medal 2014 & 15, 'The Fifty Best' Best Gin Awards – Double Gold 2016, SIP Awards – Gold 2015 & Consumers Choice Award 2015, London Spirits Competition – Silver 2020 and International Spirits Challenge – Silver 2021

Broken Heart Angel's Share Gin

40% ABV

A modern dry style gin, Broken Heart Angel's Share Gin is a collectors edition made in small batches that play on the frontiers of balance with its botanicals.

DISTILLERY:
Broken Heart Spirits,
Arrow Junction

BOTANICALS:
Juniper, Coriander, Citrus, Angelica, Lavender, Orange Flower, Hops, Ginger, Pimento, Cinnamon, Orange Peel, Thyme, Rosemary & Hemp

---

TASTING NOTES:
Herbacious and earthy on the nose, green and lemony on the palate with peppery heat. Medium finish.

SERVING SUGGESTION:
Enjoy with Fever-Tree Mediterranean Tonic Water and a sprig of rosemary.

AWARDS:
NZ Spirit Awards – Gold 2020 & Silver 2021

Broken Heart Gin

40% ABV

A modern dry style gin, Broken Heart Original Gin balances earthy, floral, spicy, and fresh flavour profiles to capture the essence of a dry Central Otago summer.

DISTILLERY:

Broken Heart Spirits,
Arrow Junction

BOTANICALS:

Juniper, Coriander, Citrus, Angelica, Lavender, Orange Flower, Hops, Ginger, Pimento & Cinnamon

---

TASTING NOTES:

Juniper and citrus on the nose, dry pepper and spice on the palate, warming, earthy spice on the finish.

SERVING SUGGESTION:

Enjoy with Fever-Tree Mediterranean Tonic Water and a slice of orange.

AWARDS:

NZ Spirit Awards — Double Gold 2020 & Silver 2021 and IWSC — Silver 2016, 2017 & 2020

Broken Heart Queenstown Edition
40% ABV

A modern dry style gin, Broken Heart Queenstown Edition was created in celebration of their 9th birthday by combining the botanical essences of their Navy Gin with the alcohol content of their Original Gin.

DISTILLERY:

Broken Heart Spirits,
Arrow Junction

BOTANICALS:

Juniper, Coriander, Citrus,
Angelica, Lavender, Orange
Flower, Hops, Ginger, Pimento
& Cinnamon

TASTING NOTES:

Very traditional botanical nose
with lots of citrus and green herb
on the palate, some piney juniper
and a soft finish.

SERVING SUGGESTION:

Enjoy with Fever-Tree
Mediterranean Tonic Water
and a slice of lemon.

AWARDS:

NZ Spirit Awards – Gold 2021

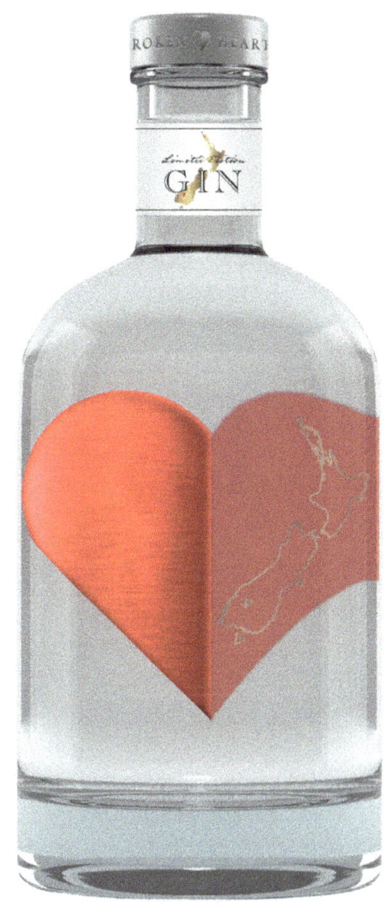

The Cardrona
DISTILLERY
NEW ZEALAND

The Source Gin

47% ABV

A modern dry style gin, The Source Gin includes locally foraged rosehip among its botanicals, which was first brought to the Cardrona Valley by Chinese immigrants during the gold rush.

DISTILLERY:
Cardrona Distillery, Cardrona

BOTANICALS:
Juniper, Rosehip, Angelica Root, Coriander Seed, Lemon Zest & Orange Zest

TASTING NOTES:
Floral nose underpinned by juniper, rosehip and delicate citrus on the palate rounding out the grain character with tropical notes of banana and spice

SERVING SUGGESTION:
Enjoy with Fever-Tree Mediterranean Tonic Water and a slice of orange.

AWARDS:
New York World Wine & Spirits Competition – Gold 2016 and 'The Fifty Best' – Gold Medal 2017

Old Jones London Dry Gin

40% ABV

A modern dry style gin, Concept Bespoke Distilling's Old Jones London Dry Gin is vegan due to using in-house, naturally distilled grain spirit and is designed to take you between a traditional London Dry and an Old Tom.

DISTILLERY:
Concept Brewing and Distilling, Christchurch

BOTANICALS:
Juniper, Cardamom, Coriander, Liquorice Root & Angelica

TASTING NOTES:
Delicate nuttiness on the nose, sweet fennel and liquorice on the palate, finishing with earthy coriander and hit of bitterness.

SERVING SUGGESTION:
Enjoy with Fever-Tree Mediterranean Tonic Water and a slice of lemon.

Curiosity Gin - Curious Dry

40% ABV

A modern dry style gin, Curious Dry is designed for the traditional gin drinker, made with the finest imported juniper and just four other botanicals all of which are native to New Zealand.

DISTILLERY:
The Spirits Workshop Distillery, Christchurch

BOTANICALS:
Juniper, Tarata, Kawakawa, Horopito & Manuka

TASTING NOTES:
Native botanicals on the nose, juniper and gentle green pepper on the palate, finish is earthy and herbaceous.

SERVING SUGGESTION:
Enjoy with Fever-Tree Mediterranean Tonic Water and a slice of lemon.

AWARDS:
Monde Awards – Gold 2017, San Francisco World Spirits Competition – Bronze 2018, SIP Awards – Silver 2018, and NZ Spirits Awards – Bronze 2020 & Silver 2021

Dancing Sands Dry Gin

44% ABV

A modern dry style gin, Dancing Sands Dry Gin is double distilled and vapour infused with eight botanicals including green manuka leaves.

DISTILLERY:
Dancing Sands Distillery, Takaka

BOTANICALS:
Juniper, Coriander Seed, Angelica Root, Manuka, Cardamom, Peppercorn, Almond & Liquorice Root

---

TASTING NOTES:
Dry, piney nose with slightly sweet nuttiness on the palate with liquorice and pepper, finishes resinous and dry.

SERVING SUGGESTION:
Enjoy with Fever-Tree Aromatic Tonic Water and a slice of lemon.

AWARDS:
San Francisco World Spirit Awards – Gold Medal 2017, Silver Medal 2018 & 19, The Gin Masters – Gold 2017 & 18, and NZ Spirits Awards – Silver 2019

Denzien Our Coast

42% ABV

A modern dry style gin, Denzien Our Coast Gin calls upon New Zealand's coastal and island identities by using native kelp and Marlborough sea salt as botanicals.

DISTILLERY:
Denzien Urban Distillery, Wellington

BOTANICALS:
Juniper, Sea Salt, Kelp, Black Cardamom, White Peppercorns, Wormwood, Coriander Seed, Angelica Root, Fennel Seed, Liquorice Root & Orris Root

TASTING NOTES:
Soft but complex pepper and juniper nose, spice and salinity on the palate with some sweet fennel and pepper on the finish.

SERVING SUGGESTION:
Enjoy with Fever-Tree Mediterranean Tonic Water and a slice of lemon.

AWARDS:
NZ Spirits Awards – Silver 2020 & Bronze 2021, San Francisco World Spirits Competition – Bronze 2020 and London Spirits Competition – Silver 2021

Denzien Te Aro Dry

42% ABV

A modern dry style gin, Denzien Te Aro Dry Gin is based on a London Dry Gin with a Kiwi twist using horopito and kawakawa.

DISTILLERY:

Denzien Urban Distillery, Wellington

BOTANICALS:

Juniper, Horopito, Kawakawa, Lemon Peel, Orange Peel, Coriander Seed, Fennel Seed, Angelica Root, Liquorice Root & Orris Root

TASTING NOTES:

Orange peel and fresh, herbacious nose opens to roasted fennel, bush pepper and a sweet, earthy base on the palate. Dry and chewy finish.

SERVING SUGGESTION:

Enjoy with Fever-Tree Premium Indian Tonic Water and a slice of lemon.

AWARDS:

NZ Spirits Awards – Trophy Winner Best New Zealand Product in Category & Best Overall in Category 2019, Gold 2019, Silver 2020 & Silver 2021, San Francisco World Spirits Competition – Bronze 2020 and London Spirits Competition – Silver 2021

Good George Day Off Gin

45% ABV

A modern dry style gin, Good George Day Off Gin is designed to evoke the concept behind its namesake and be enjoyed while relaxing.

DISTILLERY:
Good George Distillery, Hamilton

BOTANICALS:
Juniper, Coriander Seed, Angelica Root, Rosehip, Liquorice Root, Pink Peppercorns, Mandarin, Star Anise & Cardamom

TASTING NOTES:
Mandarin and pepper are bold on the nose, plenty of sweet and warming spice on the palate with pepper lingering for a dry finish.

SERVING SUGGESTION:
Enjoy with Fever-Tree Aromatic Tonic Water and a slice of lemon.

AWARDS:
NZ Spirits Awards — Silver 2020 & Gold 2021 and London Spirits Competition — Bronze 2020

Humdinger Citrus Gin

40% ABV

A modern dry style gin, Humdinger Citrus Gin is made using many of the same botanicals as their Dry Gin with a greater focus on the fresh lemon and orange peel they source from Gisborne.

DISTILLERY:
Humdinger Distillery,
Geraldine

BOTANICALS:
Juniper, Barley, Coriander,
Nutmeg, Angelica Root, Orris
Root, Ginger, Lemon Peel and
Orange Peel

TASTING NOTES:
Fresh citrus on the nose with
subtle hints of ginger and baking
spice on the palate alongside
orange peel. Dry finish.

SERVING SUGGESTION:
Enjoy with Fever-Tree
Mediterranean Tonic Water and a
slice of lemon.

AWARDS:
NZ Spirits Awards – Bronze 2021,
London Spirits Competition –
Silver 2021 and IWSC –
Bronze 2021

Humdinger Dry Gin

40% ABV

A modern dry style gin, Humdinger Dry Gin is distilled using the London Dry Method in a balance between British methodology and Humdinger's flair for ingenuity.

DISTILLERY:
Humdinger Distillery,
Geraldine

BOTANICALS:
Juniper, Barley, Coriander, Nutmeg, Liquorice Root, Angelica Root, Orris Root, Ginger, Lemon Peel & Orange Peel

---

TASTING NOTES:
Woodsy and spicy on the nose, touch of lemon balances this on the palate. Spice develops and lingers on the finish.

SERVING SUGGESTION:
Enjoy with Fever-Tree Mediterranean Tonic Water and a slice of lemon.

AWARDS:
NZ Spirits Awards – Gold 2021, London Spirits Competition – Silver 2021 and IWSC – Bronze 2021

Reikorangi Triple Distilled Dry Gin

42% ABV

A modern dry style gin, Reikorangi Triple Distilled Dry Gin aims to create a rustic craft edge with the use of whole oranges, lemons, and limes amongst other botanicals.

DISTILLERY:
imagination, Reikorangi

BOTANICALS:
Juniper, Coriander Seed, Cinnamon, Liquorice Root, Orris Root, Orange, Lime, Lemon & Manuka

---

TASTING NOTES:
Bold spice and citrus on the nose, juniper on the palate with marmalade zest and rich sweetness, anise and spice on the finish.

SERVING SUGGESTION:
Enjoy with Fever-Tree Refreshingly Light Indian Tonic Water and a slice of orange.

AWARDS:
NZ Spirits Awards – Gold 2020, SIP Awards – Gold 2019 & 20, IWSC World Awards – Bronze 2019, and London Spirit Awards – Silver 2020

Juno Extra Fine

40% ABV

A modern dry style gin, Juno Extra Fine is their signature gin made using a range of fresh, locally-grown botanicals and pure mountain water sourced from Mount Taranaki.

DISTILLERY:
Begin Distilling,
New Plymouth

BOTANICALS:
Juniper, Coriander Seed, Angelica Root, Orris Root, Kaffir Lime Leaf, Manuka, Orange, Black Peppercorns, Cardamom & Cassia

TASTING NOTES:
Complex kaffir lime, green spice and roots on the nose carries through to the palate with additional bush honey, orange peel and a dry finish.

SERVING SUGGESTION:
Enjoy with Fever-Tree Mediterranean Tonic Water and a slice of lime.

AWARDS:
San Francisco World Spirits Competition — Silver 2018 & Double Gold Packaging Design Award 2018, IWSC London — Silver 2019, Singapore World Spirits Competition — Silver 2019, SIP Awards — Silver 2020, and NZ Spirits Awards — Silver 2019, 2020 & 2021

Championz Gin

40% ABV

A modern dry style gin, Championz Gin is a dry gin made with water from the nearby Te Waikoropupu Springs, often considered the clearest spring water in the world.

DISTILLERY:
Kiwi Spirit Distillery, Motupipi

BOTANICALS:
Juniper, Angelica, Liquorice & Others

TASTING NOTES:
Mint, lemon and eucalyptus on the nose, some mint continues on the palate with some spice and citrus. Long, dry, hot finish.

SERVING SUGGESTION:
Enjoy with Fever-Tree Premium Indian Tonic Water and a slice of lemon.

AWARDS:
China Wine and Spirit Awards — Double Gold 2020 and New York World Spirit Awards -Silver 2019

Delightful Dry Gin

40% ABV

A modern dry style gin, Kiwi Spirit's Delightful Dry Gin is made using a variety of botanicals including lavender and lemon which are grown on the distillery's grounds and picked fresh.

DISTILLERY:
Kiwi Spirit Distillery,
Motupipi

BOTANICALS:
Juniper, Lavender, Lemon
& Others

TASTING NOTES:
Savoury and herbaceous character on the nose, slightly sweet earthy spice on the palate, medium finish with some baking spice.

SERVING SUGGESTION:
Enjoy with Fever-Tree Premium Indian Tonic Water and a slice of lemon.

Laughing Club Gin

44% ABV

A modern dry style gin, Laughing Club Gin takes inspiration from the roaring 20s, the luxury Raffles Hotel in Singapore, and a legend about a raucous club by the same name.

DISTILLERY:
Kiwi Spirit Distillery,
Motupipi

BOTANICALS:
Juniper, Coriander Seed,
Pepper, Cubeb, Lemon, Orris
Root, Liquorice & Others

TASTING NOTES:
Dry citrus nose, juniper and
coriander developing on the
palate with some hot pepper and
rootsy character. Short finish.

SERVING SUGGESTION:
Enjoy with Fever-Tree Premium
Indian Tonic Water and a slice
of lemon.

Lighthouse Gin Original

42% ABV

A London dry style gin, Lighthouse Gin Original's recipe was perfected over many years with a unique blend of nine botanicals and was the first ever New Zealand gin to be selected for presentation by the UK's Craft Gin Club.

DISTILLERY:
Lighthouse Distillery, Martinborough

BOTANICALS:
Juniper, Coriander Seed, Yen Ben Lemon Zest, Navel Orange Zest, Cinnamon, Almond, Cassia Bark, Orris Root & Liquorice Root

---

TASTING NOTES:
Lemon peel and baking spice on the nose, dry juniper and orange peel on the palate with gentle nuttiness. Long citrus finish.

SERVING SUGGESTION:
Enjoy with Fever-Tree Premium Indian Tonic Water and a slice of lemon.

AWARDS:
IWSC – Gold 2020 and Global Gin Masters - Master 90+ Points 2019

No8 Distillery Dunners Dry Gin

44% ABV

A modern dry style gin, the No8 Distillery Dunners Dry Gin takes cues from its two makers' culinary histories with botanicals from the Mediterranean and Aotearoa included in its blend.

DISTILLERY:
No8 Distillery,
Dunedin

BOTANICALS:
Juniper, Coriander Seed,
Angelica Root, Orris Root,
Lemon, Lime, Mandarin,
Kawakawa, Tarata, Thyme,
Basil & Sage

TASTING NOTES:
Earthy spice and native bush on the nose, bush pepper and black tea with hints of citrus on the palate. Long herbal finish.

SERVING SUGGESTION:
Enjoy with Fever-Tree Mediterranean Tonic Water and a slice of lime.

AWARDS:
NZ Spirits Awards —
Bronze 2021

Papaka Road Gin

42% ABV

A modern dry style gin, Papaka Road Gin aims to evoke the warmth, refreshment, and seclusion of the Tutukaka Coast with fresh, seasonal citrus zest and natural botanicals.

DISTILLERY:
Papaka Road Distillery,
Ngunguru

BOTANICALS:
Juniper, Coriander, Angelica,
Liquorice, Seasonal Citrus
& Others

TASTING NOTES:
Slightly sweet baking spice and
marmalade on the nose with
spice and citrus on the palate,
lingering liquorice on the finish.

SERVING SUGGESTION:
Enjoy with Fever-Tree Premium
Indian Tonic Water and a slice
of orange.

AWARDS:
NZ Spirits Awards – Bronze 2021

Pink & White - White Dry
45% ABV

A London dry style gin, Pink & White's White Dry Gin is modelled after a classic London Dry with the goal of creating a "Gin that tastes like Gin".

DISTILLERY:
Pink & White - Geothermal Gin, Rotorua

BOTANICALS:
Juniper, Coriander, Angelica Root, Lemon & Others

TASTING NOTES:
Subtle coriander on the nose, spearmint and forest floor on the palate, mild, earthy finish.

SERVING SUGGESTION:
Enjoy with Fever-Tree Mediterranean Tonic Water and a slice of lemon.

AWARDS:
NZ Spirits Awards – Double Gold 2021

Reid + Reid Native Gin

42% ABV

A modern dry style gin, Reid + Reid Native Gin is the result of a two year mission foraging the landscapes of New Zealand for the aromatic native plants that best compliment a classic dry gin, including kawakawa, manuka, and horopito.

DISTILLERY:
Reid + Reid Distillery,
Martinborough

BOTANICALS:
Juniper, Coriander Seed,
Angelica Root, Liquorice Root,
Orris Root, Fennel Seed,
Nutmeg, Cassia, Cardamom,
Orange Peel, Kawakawa,
Horopito & Manuka

TASTING NOTES:
Earthy spice and citrus peel on
the nose, kawakawa and manuka
on the palate. Sweet and
spicy finish.

SERVING SUGGESTION:
Enjoy with Fever-Tree
Mediterranean Tonic Water
and a slice of lemon.

Reid + Reid Rev. Dawson's Gin

42% ABV

A modern dry style gin, Reid + Reid Rev. Dawson's Gin is distilled using the 'one shot' method and is named tongue-in-cheek after one of New Zealand's leading prohibitionists from the early 1900's who also happens to be the brothers' great, great grandfather.

DISTILLERY:
Reid + Reid Distillery, Martinborough

BOTANICALS:
Juniper, Coriander Seed, Angelica Root, Orris Root, Fennel Seed, Cassia, Orange & Grapefruit

TASTING NOTES:
Grapefruit with coriander on the nose, marmalade on toast with hints of spice on the palate, earthy roots and some heat on the finish.

SERVING SUGGESTION:
Enjoy with Fever-Tree Premium Indian Tonic Water and a slice of grapefruit.

Rifters Original Dry Gin

42% ABV

A modern dry style gin, Rifters Original Dry Gin is made using a selection of locally foraged botanicals amongst others and presented in a bottle made from 20%+ recycled glass.

DISTILLERY:
Arrowtown Distillery,
Arrowtown

BOTANICALS:
Juniper, Coriander Seed,
Angelica Root, Liquorice
Root, Orris Root, Cinnamon,
Cardamom, Orange Peel
& Others

TASTING NOTES:
A fresh nose full of pine and citrus
delivers a touch of spice on the
palate with lingering sweet and tangy
citrus fruit on a resinous finish.

SERVING SUGGESTION:
Enjoy with Fever-Tree Premium
Indian Tonic Water and a slice
of lemon.

AWARDS:
NZ Spirits Awards – Gold 2020
& Silver 2021 and San Francisco
World Spirits Competition –
Silver 2021

Roots Marlborough Dry Gin

45% ABV

A modern dry style gin, Roots Marlborough Dry Gin is made in the style of a London Dry Gin using New Zealand native and grown botanicals including kawakawa fruit and gorse flower.

DISTILLERY:
Elemental Distillers,
Blenheim

BOTANICALS:
Juniper, Grapefruit Zest,
Coriander Seed, Hops, Kawakawa
Fruit & Gorse Flower

TASTING NOTES:
Grapefruit and kawakawa on the
nose, bitter hops, citrus peel and
juniper on the palate. Lingering
dry finish.

SERVING SUGGESTION:
Enjoy with Fever-Tree
Mediterranean Tonic Water and
a slice of grapefruit.

AWARDS:
NZ Spirits Awards – Trophy
Winner Best New Zealand Product
in Category & Best Overall in
Category 2021, Gold 2020 &
Gold 2021

The Valley Gin

42% ABV

A modern dry style gin, Ruin Distillery's The Valley Gin is made using their own grain neutral spirit fermented with champagne yeast, and infused with botanicals of which some are locally foraged.

DISTILLERY:
Ruin Distillery, Moonshine Valley

BOTANICALS:
Juniper, Coriander, Angelica Root, Liquorice Root, Fennel Seed, Orange Zest, Lemon Zest, Black Pepper, Orris Root, Cassia Bark & Kawakawa Leaves

---

TASTING NOTES:
Damp, green nose with some menthol and pepper on the palate, hints of citrus and fennel. Hot, dry finish.

SERVING SUGGESTION:
Enjoy with Fever-Tree Aromatic Tonic Water and a slice of lemon.

Lovers Leap Dry Gin

43% ABV

A modern dry style gin, Sandymount Distillery's Lovers Leap Gin is named after a nearby spot on the Otago Peninsula coastline and created as a nod to the London Dry style with a hint of New Zealand flavour.

DISTILLERY:
Sandymount Distillery,
Otago Peninsula

———

BOTANICALS:
Juniper, Angelica, Cardamom,
Coriander, Orris Root, Manuka
Flower, Lime & Lemon

———

TASTING NOTES:
Vegetal nose with coriander and
hints of citrus. Bigger citrus
on the palate with a touch of
sweetness. Slightly floral but
dry finish.

———

SERVING SUGGESTION:
Enjoy with Fever-Tree
Mediterranean Tonic Water and
a slice of lemon.

———

AWARDS:
NZ Spirits Awards – Silver 2021

Scapegrace Classic

42.2% ABV

A London dry style gin, Scapegrace Classic epitomises the nature of a classic gin, made using 12 botanicals of which juniper and citrus peel shine through.

DISTILLERY:
Scapegrace Distilling Co.,
Christchurch

BOTANICALS:
Juniper, Lemon Peel, Orange Peel, Coriander Seed, Cardamom, Nutmeg, Angelica Root, Liquorice Root, Orris Root, Cloves, Cinnamon & Cassia Bark

---

TASTING NOTES:
Dry citrus on the nose, intense citrus on the palate with warming spice. Bright, clean and short finish.

SERVING SUGGESTION:
Enjoy with Fever-Tree Premium Indian Tonic Water and a slice of orange.

AWARDS:
San Francisco World Spirits Competition – Double Gold 2014, Gin Masters – Gold 2018, and London International Wines & Spirits Competition – Outstanding Silver 2014, Silver 2018 & Gold 2020

Solace Dry Gin

42.2 % ABV

A classic style gin, Solace Dry Gin is triple distilled and pays homage to the London Dry Gin style using a mixture of 13 traditional botanicals.

DISTILLERY:
Kings Liquor, Auckland

BOTANICALS:
Juniper, Coriander Seed, Cassia Bark, Angelica Root, Nutmeg, Citrus Peel, Tangerine, Orris Root, Star Anise, Anise, Lemon, Orange & Cardamon

---

TASTING NOTES:
Spirit-forward, grassy and citrus nose, sweet and round citrus on the palate finishes dry with a hint of earthy spices.

SERVING SUGGESTION:
Enjoy with Fever-Tree Premium Indian Tonic Water and a slice of lemon.

Twelfth Hour Dry Gin

43% ABV

A modern dry style gin, Twelfth Hour Dry Gin is the final result after 22 previous iterations and made using homegrown Makrut (Kaffir Lime).

DISTILLERY:
Twelfth Hour Distillery,
Auckland

BOTANICALS:
Juniper, Coriander Orange,
Lemon, Kaffir Lime & Others

TASTING NOTES:
Kaffir lime and juniper on the
nose, green coriander seed, mint
and pine on the palate with a
slightly hot, dry finish.

SERVING SUGGESTION:
Enjoy with Fever-Tree
Mediterranean Tonic Water
and a slice of lime.

AWARDS:
NZ Spirit Awards – Silver 2021

The Vicar's Son Gin — Classic London Dry
46% ABV

A London dry style gin, The Vicar's Son Gin Classic London Dry is quadruple distilled with 20 vapour infusion extraction cycles and uses Antipodes Water throughout their process.

DISTILLERY:
The Vicar's Son,
Auckland

BOTANICALS:
Juniper, Lemon Peel, Lime Peel, Nutmeg, Red Pepper, Green Pepper, Almond, Cinnamon, Cardamom, Poppy Seed, Liquorice, Coriander & Angelica

---

TASTING NOTES:
Intense lemon and pepper nose, soft cardamom opens to bold lemon, grassiness and spice on the palate. Hints of pine on the finish.

SERVING SUGGESTION:
Enjoy with Fever-Tree Refreshingly Light Indian Tonic Water and a slice of lemon

---

AWARDS:
NZ Spirits Awards — Silver 2021

Victor Gin Original

42% ABV

A modern dry style gin, Victor Gin Original looks to early rock n' roll and the idea of using only a few instruments that sound great together by using only the flavours that they love rather than a broad range of botanicals.

DISTILLERY:
Thomson Whisky Distillery, Riverhead

BOTANICALS:
Juniper, Lemon, Lemongrass, Cardamom & Coriander Seed

TASTING NOTES:
Juniper and citrus led nose, sweet mid-palate and vibrant, herbaceous notes of lemongrass, lemon and coriander. Dry, citrus finish.

SERVING SUGGESTION:
Enjoy with Fever-Tree Mediterranean Tonic Water and a slice of lemon.

AWARDS:
San Francisco World Spirits Competition — Double Gold 2019 and NZ Spirits Awards — Silver 2020

Waiheke Distilling Co. London Dry Gin

42% ABV

A modern dry style gin, Waiheke Distilling Co.'s London Dry Gin is based on the time-honoured classic with notable additions of macadamia and pink peppercorn.

DISTILLERY:
Waiheke Distilling Co.,
Waiheke

BOTANICALS:
Juniper, Macadamia, Pink
Peppercorn, Lemon & Others

TASTING NOTES:
Fragrant, nutty nose with lemon
and juniper. Slightly sweet with
a hot pepper on the palate and
earthy, dry finish.

SERVING SUGGESTION:
Enjoy with Fever-Tree Premium
Indian Tonic Water and a slice
of lemon.

AWARDS:
NZ Spirits Awards —
Silver 2021

Waiheke Distilling Co. Spirit of Waiheke

42% ABV

A modern dry style gin, Waiheke Distilling Co.'s Spirit of Waiheke is designed to pay homage to its island provenance, embodying the land, wind, and sea around Waiheke.

DISTILLERY:
Waiheke Distilling Co.,
Waiheke

BOTANICALS:
Juniper & Others

TASTING NOTES:
Citrus and green bush herb on the nose, minerality, lemon and vegetal quality on the palate, astringent with hints of olive leaf on the finish.

SERVING SUGGESTION:
Enjoy with Fever-Tree Refreshingly Light Indian Tonic Water and a slice of lime.

AWARDS:
NZ Spirits Awards —
Bronze 2021

Waitoki Gin

43% ABV

A modern dry style gin, Waitoki Gin was born out of 40 different recipes over the course of 18 months, combining traditional botanicals with native kawakawa and horopito, fresh orange and grapefruit, and additions from a local tree that is 200+ years old.

DISTILLERY:
Washhouse Distillery, Waitoki

BOTANICALS:
Juniper, Coriander Seed, Angelica Root, Orange, Grapefruit, Kawakawa, Horopito & Others

---

TASTING NOTES:
Grapefruit peel and native green leaf on the nose, orange sweetness, root spice and pepper dominate the palate with a very dry and hot finish.

SERVING SUGGESTION:
Enjoy with Fever-Tree Aromatic Tonic Water and a slice of grapefruit.

AWARDS:
NZ Spirits Awards – Silver 2020 & Silver 2021 and The Junipers New Zealand Gin Awards – Bronze 2020

ALBERTINE
GIN
NATURE IS THE MEASURE
HASTINGS DISTILLERS
NEW ZEALAND
THE
DOYENNE
GIN
WELLINGTON
GIN
DISTILLED AND BOTTLED BY HAND
Batch no: 0037
70CL
41% ALC/VOL.
BUREAUCRATS GIN LTD
VICTOR GIN
V
NEW ZEALAND
EAST BLOCK 200
GIN
HASTINGS DISTILLERS
NEW ZEALAND

CONTEMPORARY

CONTEMPORARY DRY

Still juniper forward, unsweetened gins that may draw on modern botanicals as well.

CONTEMPORARY MODERN

These are gins that still include juniper in the botanical profile but are not juniper forward relying on other modern botanicals to create unique flavour profiles.

____

Ariki Ultra Premium Gin

45% ABV

A contemporary modern style gin, Ariki Ultra Premium Gin is a smooth collaboration of pure New Zealand water and unique Pacific botanicals including Rarotongan vanilla and Tongan coconut.

DISTILLERY:
Ariki Spirit, Mount Maunganui

BOTANICALS:
Juniper, Almond, Coriander Seed, Angelica Root, Orange Peel, Orris Root, Lemon Peel, Liquorice Root, Black Pepper, Cardamom, Manuka Flower, Cinnamon, Lemon Grass, Vanilla & Coconut

TASTING NOTES:
Coconut, vanilla and marzipan on the nose with lots of creaminess and sweet orange on the palate before a big, bold black pepper finish.

SERVING SUGGESTION:
Enjoy with Fever-Tree Mediterranean Tonic Water and a slice of lemon.

Awildian Coromandel Dry Gin

47% ABV

A contemporary dry gin, Awildian Coromandel Dry Gin is made using 20 botanicals and water from the Coromandel Ranges and then rested for three weeks before a final reduction to its bottling strength of 47% ABV.

DISTILLERY:
Coromandel Distilling Co.,
Thames

BOTANICALS:
Juniper, Rose, Coriander, Angelica, Hibiscus, Blueberry, Cubeb, Lemon, Orange, Grapefruit, Orris, Lemon Thyme, Liquorice & Others

TASTING NOTES:
Floral, earthy and subtle citrus on the nose, slightly sweet palate of orange, pepper and spice. Soft, round finish.

SERVING SUGGESTION:
Enjoy with Fever-Tree Refreshingly Light Indian Tonic Water and a slice of lemon.

AWARDS:
San Francisco World Spirits Awards – Silver 2021, NZ Spirits Awards – Silver 2021, and Dish Magazine Tasting Panel – Top Pick 2021

Awildian Coromandel Dry Gin — Blue Edition
47% ABV

A contemporary dry gin, Awildian Coromandel Dry Gin - Blue Edition uses their Coromandel Dry Gin as its base with the addition of butterfly pea flowers which gives it its rich purple blue colour.

DISTILLERY:
Coromandel Distilling Co.,
Thames

BOTANICALS:
Juniper, Rose, Coriander, Butterfly Pea Flower, Angelica, Hibiscus, Blueberry, Cubeb, Lemon, Orange, Grapefruit, Orris, Lemon Thyme, Liquorice & Others.

TASTING NOTES:
Floral, earthy nose with slight bitterness of butterfly pea flower. Soft, slightly sweet citrus and spice on the palate, soft finish.

SERVING SUGGESTION:
Enjoy with Fever-Tree Refreshingly Light Indian Tonic Water and a slice of lemon.

The Bond Store Kawakawa Gin

37.5% ABV

A contemporary modern style gin, The Bond Store Kawakawa Gin is made using a selection of botanicals including kawakawa grown on the family farm in rural Wairarapa.

DISTILLERY:
Koakoa, Paraparaumu

BOTANICALS:
Juniper, Kawakawa & Others

TASTING NOTES:
Kawakawa, citrus and faint cinnamon on the nose with candy-sweet lemon and pepper on the palate before a spicy, dry finish.

SERVING SUGGESTION:
Enjoy with Fever-Tree Mediterranean Tonic Water and a slice of lemon.

AWARDS:
NZ Spirits Awards – Bronze 2020 and Cathay Pacific Hong Kong International Wine and Spirit Competition – Bronze 2019

Bureaucrats: The Bureaucrat

41% ABV

A contemporary modern style gin, Bureaucrats: The Bureaucrat has a combination of ten botanicals with a focus on bold spice flavours and sweet undertones.

DISTILLERY:
Bureaucrats Gin Ltd.,
Wellington

BOTANICALS:
Juniper, Coriander Seed,
Cinnamon & Others

TASTING NOTES:
Classic baking spice and ginger on the nose, with some sweetness on the palate before a slightly bitter finish full of coriander and cinnamon.

SERVING SUGGESTION:
Enjoy with Fever-Tree Aromatic Tonic Water and a slice of lemon.

AWARDS:
NZ Spirits Awards — Silver 2020 & Bronze 2021

Bureaucrats: The Doyenne

41% ABV

A contemporary modern style gin, The Doyenne uses a unique combination of botanicals, including coconut, lime, and zesty lemongrass.

DISTILLERY:
Bureaucrats Gin Ltd.,
Wellington

BOTANICALS:
Juniper, Coriander Seed,
Coconut, Lime, Lemongrass
& Others

TASTING NOTES:
Savoury lemongrass and lime
on the nose with a soft coconut
creaminess and fresh coriander on
the palate. A long, limey finish.

SERVING SUGGESTION:
Enjoy with Fever-Tree
Mediterranean Tonic Water and a
slice of lime.

AWARDS:
NZ Spirits Awards — Gold 2020

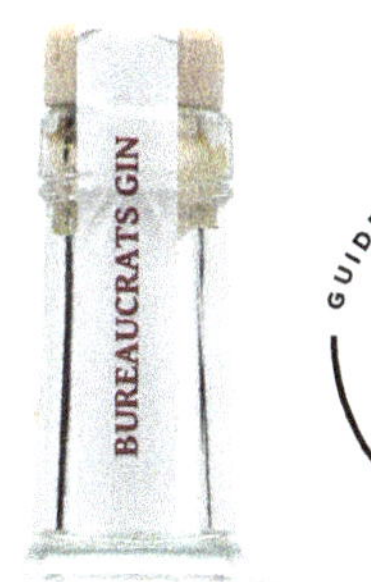

Curiosity Gin - Recipe #23

42% ABV

A contemporary modern style gin, Curiosity Gin - Recipe #23 is made using a base spirit distilled in-house from Canterbury malted barley and 11 botanicals including a generous helping of East Coast manuka, fresh citrus, and Otago lavender.

DISTILLERY:
The Spirits Workshop Distillery, Christchurch

BOTANICALS:
Juniper, Manuka Berries & Leaves, Coriander Seed, Cardamom, Orange Zest, Lime Zest, Ginger Root, Angelica Root, Lavender, Cinnamon & Star Anise

TASTING NOTES:
Fresh pine and sweet herb on the nose, with more spice and citrus on the palate. Lots of ginger and anise on a lingering finish.

SERVING SUGGESTION:
Enjoy with Fever-Tree Mediterranean Tonic Water and a slice of orange.

AWARDS:
Monde Awards – Gold 2017, San Francisco World Spirits Competition – Bronze 2018, SIP Awards – Silver 2018, and NZ Spirits Awards – Bronze 2020

Denzien Smoke & Embers

44% ABV

A contemporary modern style gin, Denzien Smoke & Embers Gin is designed to mimic some of the qualities of whiskey by including morita, chipotle, and habanero chillies as botanicals.

DISTILLERY:
Denzien Urban Distillery, Wellington

BOTANICALS:
Juniper, Morita, Chipotle, Guajillo, California, Mulato Negro & Habanero Chillies, Coriander Seed, Angelica Root, Fennel Seed, Liquorice Root & Orris Root

---

TASTING NOTES:
Smoke and chilli on the nose with subtle heat, fennel and root spice on the palate before a fennel and aniseed driven finish.

SERVING SUGGESTION:
Enjoy with Fever-Tree Smoky Ginger Ale and a slice of orange.

AWARDS:
NZ Spirits Awards – Bronze 2020, Silver 2021 and London Spirits Competition – Bronze 2021

Dr Beak

Dr Beak New Zealand Garden Gin

45.5% ABV

A contemporary dry gin, Dr Beak New Zealand Garden Gin was designed around their seven core botanicals to be fresh and sprightly like the Piwakawaka, or Fantail.

DISTILLERY:
Elemental Distillers,
Marlborough

BOTANICALS:
Juniper, Coriander Seed, Orris Root, Bay Leaf, Horopito, Rosemary & Mint

TASTING NOTES:
Fresh and green nose of savoury herb, pepper and mint. Savoury palate with a bright minty note before finishing with long, dry juniper.

SERVING SUGGESTION:
Enjoy with Fever-Tree Mediterranean Tonic Water and a sprig of mint.

AWARDS:
NZ Spirit Awards — Silver 2021

Dr Beak

Dr Beak New Zealand Premium Gin
48% ABV

A contemporary modern gin, Dr Beak New Zealand Premium Gin is bursting with flavour due to the high number of essential oils and will cloud up when left in the freezer or mixed with tonic.

DISTILLERY:
Elemental Distillers, Marlborough

BOTANICALS:
Juniper, Coriander Seed, Lavender, Mint, Chamomile, Lemon Verbena, Orris Root, Thyme, Rosemary, Lime Peel, Kelp, Horopito & Bay Leaf

TASTING NOTES:
Herbaceous green and damp nose with grassy quality. Lime and root spice on the palate with a damp vegetal finish.

SERVING SUGGESTION:
Enjoy with Fever-Tree Mediterranean Tonic Water and a sprig of rosemary.

AWARDS:
NZ Spirit Awards – Gold 2021 and London Spirits Competition – Silver 2021

Eliza's Claim Dry Gin

47% ABV

A contemporary dry style gin, Eliza's Claim Dry Gin is named in memory of a pioneering goldmine in the Kaimai Ranges with gold flakes to reflect the heritage of the area where it is made.

DISTILLERY:
Kaimai Brewing & Distilling Co.,
Waikino

BOTANICALS:
Juniper, Angelica, Rosemary,
Manuka Honey & Others

TASTING NOTES:
Rosemary and honey on the nose,
savoury heat opens up on the
palate with juicy chile and herbs,
a lingering spicy finish.

SERVING SUGGESTION:
Enjoy with Fever-Tree
Mediterranean Tonic Water and a
sprig of rosemary.

Eliza's Claim Gold Gin

47% ABV

A contemporary dry style gin, Eliza's Claim Gold Gin combines 12 botanicals with 50,000-year-old water from an artesian aquifer in the Coromandel Ranges and gold flakes resulting in a pale golden colour.

DISTILLERY:
Kaimai Brewing & Distilling Co., Waikino

BOTANICALS:
Juniper, Citrus, Rosemary, Manuka Honey & Others

TASTING NOTES:
Soft and floral nose of herbaceous flowers and honey. Sweet, green herbs on the palate with warming finish.

SERVING SUGGESTION:
Enjoy with Fever-Tree Mediterranean Tonic Water and a slice of lemon.

AWARDS:
NZ Spirit Awards – Gold 2021

EXHIBIT A
(Est. 2020)

Exhibit A No. 580

42% ABV

A contemporary dry style gin, Exhibit A No. 580 is made using collected rainwater and a vegan base spirit all presented in a bottle handmade by sculptor Gidon Bing.

DISTILLERY:
imagaination,
Reikorangi

BOTANICALS:
Juniper, Citrus, Green Tea,
Cardamom & Others

TASTING NOTES:
Menthol and green spices on the nose with lots of heat and lemon peel on the palate before a clean finish with notes of green tea.

SERVING SUGGESTION:
Enjoy with Fever-Tree Refreshingly Light Indian Tonic Water and a slice of lemon.

AWARDS:
NZ Spirit Awards – Silver 2021

1564 Venus and Adonis

40% ABV

A contemporary dry style gin, Fenton Street's 1564 Venus & Adonis Shakespeare's Gin is named for the poet's most popular poem with botanicals selected to represent each of the lovers and their story.

DISTILLERY:
Fenton Street Distillery,
Stratford

BOTANICALS:
Juniper, Kawakawa, Angelica, Coriander, Rose Petal, Citrus, Dandelion Root, Rimu & Miro Berries

---

TASTING NOTES:
Piney, resinous green wood and kawakawa with plenty of pepper and bitter roots on the palate before a hot, dry finish.

SERVING SUGGESTION:
Enjoy with Fever-Tree Mediterranean Tonic Water and a slice of lemon.

AWARDS:
NZ Spirit Awards – Bronze 2021

The Artist

40% ABV

A contemporary modern style gin, The Artist is triple distilled with horopito and ginger alongside a range of other botanicals with the aim of producing a gin that appeals to whisky drinkers.

DISTILLERY:
Fenton Street Distillery, Stratford

BOTANICALS:
Juniper, Kawakawa, Angelica, Coriander, Oak Wine Staves, Tarata, Horopito, Citrus, Pepper, Ginger, Cassia Bark, Nutmeg, Honey & Manuka

TASTING NOTES:
Ginger, horopito, pepper and green kawakawa on the nose with lots of green spice and lemon on the palate before a hot, bitter finish.

SERVING SUGGESTION:
Enjoy with Fever-Tree Premium Indian Tonic Water and a slice of lemon.

AWARDS:
The Junipers — Bronze 2020 and Dish Magazine Tasting Panel — Top Pick 2021

The Novelist

40% ABV

A contemporary modern style gin, The Novelist uses bush honey from eastern Taranaki to draw together its other botanicals into a smooth yet complex gin.

DISTILLERY:
Fenton Street Distillery, Stratford

BOTANICALS:
Juniper, Coriander, Angelica, Horopito, Black Pepper, Liquorice, Cassia Bark, Orris Root, Honey & Citrus

---

TASTING NOTES:
Honey and horopito on the nose, nutty spice and lime on the palate with horopito and liquorice on the finish.

SERVING SUGGESTION:
Enjoy with Fever-Tree Premium Indian Tonic Water and a slice of lemon.

AWARDS:
NZ Spirit Awards – Bronze 2020

The Poet

40% ABV

A contemporary modern style gin, The Poet celebrates the traditional character of a London Dry Gin with the inclusion of New Zealand citrus.

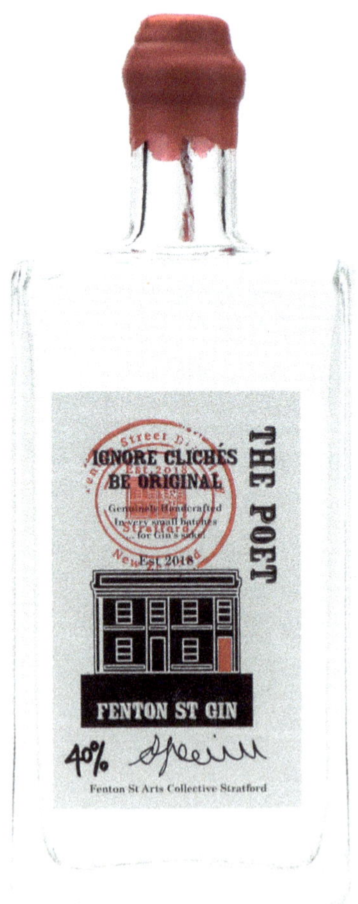

DISTILLERY:
Fenton Street Distillery, Stratford

BOTANICALS:
Juniper, Coriander, Angelica, Cardamom, Citrus & Orris Root

TASTING NOTES:
Cardamom and root spice on the nose with soft florals, citrus and green spice on the palate. A long, hot finish.

SERVING SUGGESTION:
Enjoy with Fever-Tree Mediterranean Tonic Water and a slice of lemon.

The Vintner

46% ABV

A contemporary modern style gin, The Vintner showcases tannins from oak staves that are immersed in red wine for 24 months before distillation.

DISTILLERY:
Fenton Street Distillery, Stratford

BOTANICALS:
Juniper, Kawakawa, Angelica, Coriander, Oak wine Staves, Tarata, Horopito, Citrus, Pepper, Ginger, Cassia Bark, Nutmeg & Honey

TASTING NOTES:
Oak-dominated nose with hints of piney juniper. Root spice, honey and native botanicals on the palate with a long and rich finish

SERVING SUGGESTION:
Enjoy with Fever-Tree Mediterranean Tonic Water and a slice of lemon.

AWARDS:
NZ Spirit Awards – Bronze 2021 and Dish Magazine Tasting Panel – Top Pick 2021

Grey Lynn Gin Parma Violet

40% ABV

A contemporary modern style gin, Grey Lynn Gin Parma Violet Gin is made with minimal botanicals to uphold their approach to creating bold and uncompromising tastes.

DISTILLERY:
Grey Lynn Gin,
Auckland

BOTANICALS:
Juniper, Apple, Cardamom &
Lavender

TASTING NOTES:
Lavender and cardamom on the
nose with baked apple and sea salt
caramel on the palate, a touch of
floral sweetness on the finish.

SERVING SUGGESTION:
Enjoy with Fever-Tree
Elderflower Tonic Water and a
slice of apple.

Grey Lynn Gin Signature Citrus

40% ABV

A contemporary modern style gin, Grey Lynn Gin Signature Citrus came about as the result of an intense trial and error process and includes a secret local ingredient.

DISTILLERY:
Grey Lynn Gin,
Auckland

BOTANICALS:
Juniper, Orange Peel, Fennel
Seed & Lemon Peel

TASTING NOTES:
Overripe orange and fennel on the nose with strong lemon and juniper on the palate. Slightly chalky, bitter herb finish.

SERVING SUGGESTION:
Enjoy with Fever-Tree Premium Indian Tonic Water and a slice of orange.

Albertine Gin

47% ABV

A contemporary dry style gin, Albertine Gin contains 38 organic botanicals with the goal of creating a sensory landscape of the freshness and vibrancy of New Zealand.

DISTILLERY:
Hastings Distillers, Hastings

BOTANICALS:
Juniper, Coriander Seed, Angelica, Lime Peel, Lemon Peel, Orange Peel, Kaffir Lime Leaf & Peel, Grapefruit Peel, Lemon Verbena, Lemongrass, Lavender, Chamomile, Manuka Flower, Sage, Rosemary, 5 Exotic Peppers, Mace & Selected Spices

TASTING NOTES:
Fragrant chamomile and green bush flowers with lemon zest on the nose, kaffir lime and savoury herbs on the palate, a complex and long finish.

SERVING SUGGESTION:
Enjoy with Fever-Tree Mediterranean Tonic Water and a slice of lime.

AWARDS:
IWSC Spirit — Gold 2020

East Block 200 Gin
40% ABV

A contemporary dry style gin, East Block 200 Gin contains ten organic botanicals of which nine are grown in Hawke's Bay.

DISTILLERY:
Hastings Distillers, Hastings

BOTANICALS:
Juniper, Coriander Seed, Angelica Root, Orange Peel, Lemon Peel, Kaffir Lime Peel, Cassia Bark, Feijoa Leaf, Bay Leaf & Lavender

---

TASTING NOTES:
Soft and complex green waxy leaves with citrus peel. Kaffir lime, sweet citrus and bitter juniper on the palate, a slow finish.

SERVING SUGGESTION:
Enjoy with Fever-Tree Mediterranean Tonic Water and a kaffir lime leaf.

AWARDS:
NZ Spirits Awards – Double Gold 2021 and Dish Magazine Tasting Panel – Top Pick & Gold Medal 2021

imagination Wakame Seaweed Dry Gin
42% ABV

A contemporary dry style gin, Imagination's Wakame Seaweed Dry Gin is made using wild wakame seaweed, known for its saltiness and umami flavour, foraged from the Wellington and Wairarapa coasts.

DISTILLERY:

imagination, Reikorangi

BOTANICALS:

Juniper, Coriander Seed, Cassia, Liquorice Root, Lime, Orange, Lemon, Green Cardamom, Orris Root & Wakame Seaweed

---

TASTING NOTES:

Citrus peel and root spice on the nose with citrus, cardamom, liquorice and saltiness on the palate. A long, hot finish.

SERVING SUGGESTION:

Enjoy with Fever-Tree Lime & Yuzu Soda and a slice of lime.

Island Gin Original
43.2% ABV

A contemporary dry style gin, Island Gin Original is focused on the inclusion of Great Barrier Island manuka & bush honey.

DISTILLERY:
Island Gin Distillery,
Great Barrier

BOTANICALS:
Juniper, Manuka & Bush Honey,
Coriander Seed, Lemon Myrtle
& Others

TASTING NOTES:
Strong citrus and green herb nose
with an astringent quality, lemon
myrtle, crushed spice and honey
on the palate. An earthy finish.

SERVING SUGGESTION:
Enjoy with Fever-Tree
Refreshingly Light Indian Tonic
Water and a slice of lemon.

AWARDS:
NZ Spirits Awards — Bronze 2020

Greenstone Gin

40% ABV

A contemporary dry style gin, Greenstone Gin is a blend of tradition and new ideas including native totara and kahikatea botanicals twice distilled with pure water from the nearby Te Waikoropupu Springs.

DISTILLERY:
Kiwi Spirits Distillery, Motupipi

BOTANICALS:
Juniper, Totara, Kahikatea & Others

TASTING NOTES:
Lots of ginger and root spice on the nose, sweet and dry on the palate with hints of liquorice and forest floor. Lingering baking spice and pine.

SERVING SUGGESTION:
Enjoy with Fever-Tree Mediterranean Tonic Water and a slice of lemon.

Tini Remana Gin
41% ABV

A contemporary modern style gin, Koakoa's Tini Remana Gin is inspired by New Zealand's history of making lemon based treats and the Italian lemon liqueur limoncello.

DISTILLERY:
Koakoa, Paraparaumu Beach

BOTANICALS:
Juniper & Others

TASTING NOTES:
Lemon myrtle and menthol on the nose with orange and lemon peel on the palate, touch of manuka honey sweetness. Short finish.

SERVING SUGGESTION:
Enjoy with Fever-Tree Mediterranean Tonic Water and a slice of lemon.

Lady H Gin

42% ABV

A contemporary modern style gin, Lady H Gin is made with botanicals selected for their delicate aromas and fresh florals to recall the finesse of a bygone time.

DISTILLERY:
Lady H Spirts, Auckland

BOTANICALS:
Juniper, Coriander Seed, Angelica Root, Orris Root, Cinnamon, Citrus & Others

---

TASTING NOTES:
Slightly spicy cinnamon nose with some sweet spice and coriander on the palate with a hot finish.

SERVING SUGGESTION:
Enjoy with Fever-Tree Indian Tonic Water and a slice of lemon.

AWARDS:
NZ Spirits Awards – Bronze 2020

Little Biddy Gin - Classic
40% ABV

A contemporary modern style gin, Little Biddy Gin — Classic makes use of several native botanicals including toatoa, tarata, horopito, and rimu, as well as douglas fir which are all foraged locally prior to distillation.

DISTILLERY:
Reefton Distilling Co., Reefton

BOTANICALS:
Juniper, Horopito, Tarata, Toatoa, Rimu, Douglas Fir, Angelica, Cardamom, Cassia, Coriander Seed, Lemon Peel, Liquorice & Orris Root

---

TASTING NOTES:
Resinous pine and menthol character on the nose with lemon peel, liquorice and root spice on the palate. A big foresty green finish.

SERVING SUGGESTION:
Enjoy with Fever-Tree Mediterranean Tonic Water and a slice of lemon.

AWARDS:
San Francisco World Spirits Competition — Silver 2019 & Bronze 2020, NZ Spirits Awards — Bronze 2019 & 20, and SIP Awards — Gold 2020

Little Biddy Gin - Gold Label
43% ABV

A contemporary modern style gin, Little Biddy Gin — Gold Label is characterised by its use of local grain spirit, wild water, and hand harvested native botanicals including foraged watercress, snow moss, kahikatea tips, and toatoa.

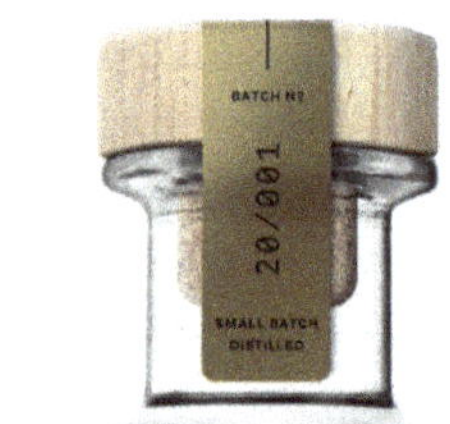

DISTILLERY:
Reefton Distilling Co., Reefton

BOTANICALS:
Juniper, Angelica Root, Caramelised Bears Limes, Cassia, Coriander Seed, Kahikatea, Liquorice Root, Nutmeg, Orris Root, Pink Peppercorns, Snow Moss, Toatoa & Watercress

---

TASTING NOTES:
Soft spice and banana, caramelised lime on the nose with elements of forest leaf and earthy spice on the palate. A hot peppery finish.

SERVING SUGGESTION:
Enjoy with Fever-Tree Mediterranean Tonic Water and a slice of lemon.

AWARDS:
NZ Spirits Awards — Bronze 2019 and The Junipers — Silver 2020

Little Biddy Gin - Black Label
46% ABV

A contemporary modern style gin, Little Biddy Gin — Black Label uses the same botanicals as their Gold Label but is designed as a sipping gin with a slightly higher alcohol by volume.

DISTILLERY:

Reefton Distilling Co.,
Reefton

BOTANICALS:

Juniper, Angelica Root, Caramelised Bears Limes, Cassia, Coriander Seed, Kahikatea, Liquorice Root, Nutmeg, Orris Root, Pink Peppercorns, Snow Moss, Toatoa & Watercress

---

TASTING NOTES:

Sweet liquorice and banana on the nose with sweet spice and forest herb and leaf on the palate. A dry finish.

SERVING SUGGESTION:

Enjoy neat or with Fever-Tree Mediterranean Tonic Water and a slice of lemon.

AWARDS:

NZ Spirits Awards — Bronze 2020, The Junipers — Silver 2020 and San Francisco World Spirits Competition — Bronze 2019

Mt. Fyffe Shearwater Gin

42% ABV

A contemporary modern style gin, Mt. Fyffe's Shearwater Gin takes inspiration from the Hutton's shearwater that nests in the local mountains and feeds in the sea by using seaweed from the local coast and blue borage from the mountains.

DISTILLERY:
Mt. Fyffe Distillery, Kaikoura

BOTANICALS:
Juniper, Coriander, Angelica Root, Rosehip, Seaweed & Blue Borage

---

TASTING NOTES:
Borage flower and seaweed bold on the nose with some sweetness balancing a salty, fresh floral palate. A sweet, dry finish.

SERVING SUGGESTION:
Enjoy with Fever-Tree Mediterranean Tonic Water and a slice of lemon.

Mt. Fyffe Woolshed Gin

42% ABV

A contemporary modern style gin, Mt. Fyffe's Woolshed Gin is named after the farm's woolshed near and around which many of the botanicals in its blend are found.

DISTILLERY:

Mt. Fyffe Distillery, Kaikoura

BOTANICALS:

Juniper, Coriander, Angelica Root, Kanuka, Mint, Elderflower, Orris Root, Cassia Bark, Nutmeg, Rosemary, Lime & Pink Peppercorn

TASTING NOTES:

Crushed mint with pepper spice on the nose, a warm baking spice with pepper on the palate before a quick finish.

SERVING SUGGESTION:

Enjoy with Fever-Tree Elderflower Tonic Water and a sprig of mint.

Adorn Beauty Gin

42% ABV

A contemporary modern style gin, Adorn Beauty Gin is inspired by the botanicals found in luxury New Zealand skincare products including New Zealand flax seed, rose petals, organic rosehip, and chamomile.

DISTILLERY:
The National Distillery Co., Napier

BOTANICALS:
Juniper, Coriander Seed, Angelica Root, Cardamom, Orris Root, Cassia Bark, Lemon Peel, Rosehip, Rose Petals, Chamomile, Flax Seed & Liquorice Root

---

TASTING NOTES:
Slightly floral notes of rose and chamomile flower on the nose. Flaxseed adds texture on the palate, chamomile, cardamom and orris are present on the long finish.

SERVING SUGGESTION:
Enjoy with Fever-Tree Elderflower Tonic Water and a slice of lemon.

AWARDS:
Australian Gin Awards – Silver 2019 & 20, The Junipers – Silver 2020, New York World Wine & Spirits Competition – Bronze 2019, SIP Awards – Platinum 2021, and London Spirit Competition – Silver 2021

Hemp Gin

45% ABV

A contemporary modern style gin, Hemp Gin expands on NDC's signature seven core gin aromatics by adding toasted hemp hearts and lashings of lemon peel.

DISTILLERY:
The National Distillery Co., Napier

BOTANICALS:
Juniper, Coriander Seed, Angelica Root, Manuka, Cardamom, Peppercorn, Almond, Liquorice Root, Hemp & Lemon Peel

TASTING NOTES:
Herbacious and green spice nose with pepper, cardamom and lemon zest on the palate. A deep and dark finish with liquorice.

SERVING SUGGESTION:
Enjoy with Fever-Tree Refreshingly Light Indian Tonic Water and a slice of lemon.

AWARDS:
NZ Spirits Awards — Trophy Winner Best New Zealand Product in Category 2020 and Best Overall in Category 2020, Gold 2020 and Bronze 2021, San Francisco World Spirits Competition — Silver 2020 & Bronze 2021 and SIP Awards — Bronze 2020 & Double Gold 2021

Meow Lucky Gin

44% ABV

A contemporary modern style gin, Meow Lucky Gin was inspired by a love of Asian cuisine incorporating yuzu, sichuan pepper, and gingko leaf into its botanical blend.

DISTILLERY:
The National Distillery Co., Napier

BOTANICALS:
Juniper, Coriander Seed, Angelica Root, Cardamom, Orris Root, Cassia Bark, Lemon Peel, Flax Seed, Liquorice Root, Yuzu, Sichuan Pepper & Ginkgo Leaf

TASTING NOTES:
Damp forest and flax with hints of citrus on the nose, flaxseed, pepper and lemon on the palate. A peppery, rootsy finish.

SERVING SUGGESTION:
Enjoy with Fever-Tree Refreshingly Light Indian Tonic Water and a slice of lemon.

AWARDS:
NZ Spirits Awards – Bronze 2021

New Zealand Dry Gin

44% ABV

A contemporary dry style gin, NDC's New Zealand Dry Gin is made using classic botanicals like coriander seed and cassia bark alongside others including lemon peel.

DISTILLERY:
The National Distillery Co.,
Napier

BOTANICALS:
Juniper, Coriander Seed,
Angelica Root, Cardamom, Orris
Root, Cassia Bark, Lemon Peel &
Liquorice Root

TASTING NOTES:
Earthy root botanicals on the
nose, resinous juniper, a touch
of lemon and bitter peel on the
palate with a peppery, long finish.

SERVING SUGGESTION:
Enjoy with Fever-Tree
Mediterranean Tonic Water and a
slice of lemon.

AWARDS:
NZ Spirits Awards – Gold 2021

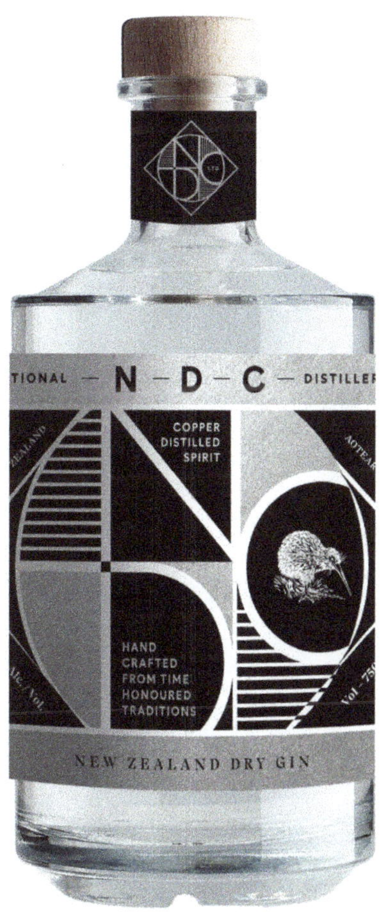

NZ Native Gin - The Proof
44% ABV

A contemporary modern style gin, NZ Native Gin - The Proof expands on NDC's signature seven core gin aromatics by showcasing native kawakawa and karamu berries.

DISTILLERY:
The National Distillery Co., Napier

BOTANICALS:
Juniper, Coriander Seed, Angelica Root, Cardamom, Orris Root, Cassia Bark, Lemon Peel, Hemp, Flax Seed, Kawakawa, Karamu & Liquorice Root

TASTING NOTES:
Earthy spice on the nose, bush pepper and liquorice on the palate before a finish of black tea and green forest floor.

SERVING SUGGESTION:
Enjoy with Fever-Tree Mediterranean Tonic Water and a slice of lemon.

AWARDS:
The Junipers – Gold 2020, Best in Class (Contemporary) 2020 and Best New Zealand Gin 2020, NZ Spirits Awards – Bronze 2021, San Francisco World Spirits Competition – Silver 2021, and London Spirit Competition – Silver 2021

Verdigris New Zealand Dry Gin

42% ABV

A contemporary dry style gin, Verdigris New Zealand Dry Gin is inspired by London Dry Gin and highlights native New Zealand flax seed among its botanicals.

DISTILLERY:
The National Distillery Co., Napier

BOTANICALS:
Juniper, Coriander Seed, Angelica Root, Cardamom, Orris Root, Cassia Bark, Lemon Peel, Flax Seed & Liquorice Root

---

TASTING NOTES:
Tart citrus nose, vibrant coriander and cardamom, spice on the palate with oily flaxseed and a nutty, earthy finish.

SERVING SUGGESTION:
Enjoy with Fever-Tree Mediterranean Tonic Water and a slice of lemon.

AWARDS:
NZ Spirits Awards – Bronze 2020 and Gold 2021, Sip Awards – Double Gold 2020 & 2021, London Spirit Competition – Silver 2020 & 2021 and San Francisco World Spirits Competition – Silver 2021

No8 Distillery Hibiscus Gin
42% ABV

A contemporary modern style gin, the No8 Distillery Hibiscus Gin is inspired by many years travelling, working, eating, and drinking in Asia and imparted with a ruby red colour by the inclusion of hibiscus petals.

DISTILLERY:
No8 Distillery, Dunedin

BOTANICALS:
Juniper , Coriander Seed, Angelica Root, Orris Root, Hibiscus, Dry Orange Bitter, Mandarin, Yuzu, Kaffir Lime Leaf, Cardamom, Cinnamon, Ginger, Passion Fruit & Gorse Flower

TASTING NOTES:
Bittersweet marmalade on the nose with hints of wild gorse, tea like astringency on the palate with hot spice before an earthy finish.

SERVING SUGGESTION:
Enjoy with Fever-Tree Mediterranean Tonic Water and a slice of lemon.

AWARDS:
NZ Spirits Awards – Silver 2021 and London Spirits Competition – Bronze 2021

No8 Distillery Horopito Fire Gin

42% ABV

A contemporary modern style gin, the No8 Distillery Horopito Fire Gin
is the result of many years of development using horopito foraged in the
Silver Peaks northwest of Dunedin.

DISTILLERY:
No8 Distillery, Dunedin

BOTANICALS:
Juniper, Coriander Seed, Angelica
Root, Orris Root, Orange,
Cardamom, Cinnamon &
Horopito Leaf

TASTING NOTES:
Piney juniper and spice on the
nose with lots of green spice and
horopito on the palate before a
baking spice finish.

SERVING SUGGESTION:
Enjoy with Fever-Tree
Mediterranean Tonic Water and a
slice of lemon.

AWARDS:
NZ Spirits Awards – Silver 2021

Rifters Quartz Gin

42% ABV

A contemporary dry style gin, Rifters Quartz Gin is distilled in small batches with locally foraged wild thyme, manuka, and douglas fir amongst other botanicals.

DISTILLERY:
Arrowtown Distillery,
Arrowtown

BOTANICALS:
Juniper, Elderberries, Mint Tips,
Thyme, Manuka, Douglas Fir
& Others

TASTING NOTES:
Mint, pine resin and savoury herb
on the nose with rosemary, wood
spice and pepper on the palate
before a spicy finish.

SERVING SUGGESTION:
Enjoy with Fever-Tree
Mediterranean Tonic Water and a
slice of lemon.

AWARDS:
NZ Spirits Awards – Silver 2021
and San Francisco World Spirits
Competition – Gold 2021

1743 Riot

42% ABV

A contemporary dry style gin, 1743 Riot is a modern take on the traditional London Dry style paying homage to the London Gin Riots of 1743 and the bold, herbaceous flavours of that era.

DISTILLERY:
Riot & Rose Spirits, Blenheim

BOTANICALS:
Juniper & Others

TASTING NOTES:
Liquorice and herbaceous aromas on the nose, subtle spice and juniper on the palate. Hints of citrus on the finish.

SERVING SUGGESTION:
Enjoy with Fever-Tree Premium Indian Tonic Water and a slice of orange.

1920 Rose

42% ABV

A contemporary modern style gin, 1920 Rose harks back to the romance and glamour of the Roaring Twenties and the flavours that saw gin come into vogue during that era including rose petal and cinnamon.

DISTILLERY:
Riot & Rose Spirits, Blenheim

BOTANICALS:
Juniper & Others

TASTING NOTES:
Manuka and juniper on the nose, with soft florals and cardamom on the palate with a long liquorice finish.

SERVING SUGGESTION:
Enjoy with Fever-Tree Elderflower Tonic Water and a slice of cucumber.

Scapegrace Black

41.6% ABV

A contemporary modern style gin, Scapegrace Black is the world's first black gin. Achieved through the use of aronia berry, saffron, pineapple, butterfly pea flower, and sweet potato, when paired with tonic its colour changes from black to purple.

DISTILLERY:

Scapegrace Distilling Co., Christchurch

BOTANICALS:

Juniper, Aronia Berry, Sweet Potato, Butterfly Pea Flower, Saffron, Pineapple & Others

TASTING NOTES:

A fresh pineapple and juniper nose with a touch of savoury sweetness on the palate before berry fruit and a sweet, dry finish.

SERVING SUGGESTION:

Enjoy with Fever-Tree Lemon Tonic Water and a slice of green apple.

GUIDE TO NEW ZEALAND GIN

STORM Black Wolf Gin

44% ABV

A contemporary modern style gin, STORM Black Wolf Gin is a collaboration between STORM clothing and The National Distillery Co. made with lashings of lemon and lime peel.

DISTILLERY:
The National Distillery Co., Napier

BOTANICALS:
Juniper, Orris Root, Angelica Root, Liquorice, Cassia Bark, Cardamon, Harakeke, Lemon Peel & Lime Peel

---

TASTING NOTES:
Earthy, forest floor nose with coriander and hints of lemon zest. Plenty of black pepper and lemon on the palate with a clean, quick finish.

SERVING SUGGESTION:
Enjoy with Fever-Tree Mediterranean Tonic Water and a slice of lemon.

AWARDS:
NZ Spirits Awards - Bronze 2021

Strange Nature Gin

44% ABV

A contemporary modern style gin, Strange Nature Gin is a grape-based gin made using alcohol extracted from sauvignon blanc wine using spinning cone technology that preserves aromas and flavours.

DISTILLERY:
The Spirits Workshop Distillery, Christchurch

BOTANICALS:
Juniper

TASTING NOTES:
Stonefruit, passionfruit, lime and damp, cut grass on the nose with caramelized, baked apricots and juniper on the palate. A lime-driven long finish.

SERVING SUGGESTION:
Enjoy over ice or with Fever-Tree Premium Soda Water.

Takapuna Gin Butterfly Pea Flower Gin

40% ABV

A contemporary modern style gin, Takapuna Butterfly Pea Flower Gin is imparted with a bright blue colour from its namesake botanical but shifts to a pink when tonic is added.

DISTILLERY:
CarbonSix Distillery,
Auckland

BOTANICALS:
Juniper, Butterfly Pea Flower
& Others

TASTING NOTES:
Cinnamon and aniseed on the
nose, some anise and spice on
the palate with a pronounced
chalkiness on the finish.

SERVING SUGGESTION:
Enjoy with Fever-Tree Premium
Indian Tonic Water and a slice
of lemon.

AWARDS:
NZ Spirits Awards - Bronze 2021

Carbon6 Black Gin

40% ABV

A contemporary modern style gin, CarbonSix Black Gin is nicknamed the "Dark Side of Gin" and made using 30 different botanicals that give it a black colour with the aim of testing the border between gins and liqueurs.

DISTILLERY:
CarbonSix Distillery,
Auckland

BOTANICALS:
Juniper & Others

TASTING NOTES:
Blackberry, raspberry and kola nut on the nose with cinnamon, star anise and sweetness on the palate before a bitter orange finish.

SERVING SUGGESTION:
Enjoy with Fever-Tree Spiced Orange Ginger Ale and a slice of orange.

AWARDS:
NZ Spirits Awards - Silver 2021

GUIDE TO NEW ZEALAND GIN

Victor Gin Kaffir Lime

42% ABV

A contemporary dry style gin, Victor Gin Kaffir Lime expands on their Original gin's core flavours and concept with the single addition of kaffir lime in its botanicals.

DISTILLERY:
Thomson Whisky Distillery, Riverhead

BOTANICALS:
Juniper, Lemon, Lemongrass, Cardamom, Coriander Seed & Kaffir Lime

---

TASTING NOTES:
Bright lemongrass, kaffir lime and soft green herbs on the nose, citrus peel and round, warm spices on the palate with a peppery, sweet finish.

SERVING SUGGESTION:
Enjoy with Fever-Tree Mediterranean Tonic Water and a slice of lime.

AWARDS:
Dish Magazine Tasting Panel — Top 5 Pick and Gold Medal 2021

Wild Diamond Black Gin

42% ABV

A contemporary modern style gin, Wild Diamond Black Gin uses their Rare Dry Gin as a base infused with additional botanicals including dutch cocoa imparting an inky black colour.

DISTILLERY:
Wild Diamond Distillery, Queenstown

BOTANICALS:
Juniper, Coriander Seed, Angelica Root, Cassia, Liquorice Extract, Orris Root, Cardamom, Chamomile, Lavender, Hypericum, Rosehip, Astragalus, Elderflower, Cocoa & Others

---

TASTING NOTES:
Strong cacao nib on the nose with vanilla cake batter that continues on the palate with hints of coffee. A dry, short finish.

SERVING SUGGESTION:
Enjoy neat or with Fever-Tree Ginger Ale.

GUIDE TO NEW ZEALAND GIN

Wild Diamond Rare Dry Gin

42% ABV

A contemporary dry style gin, Wild Diamond Rare Dry Gin is a limited edition premium batch with botanicals including rosehip, elderflower, lavender, and astragalus.

DISTILLERY:
Wild Diamond Distillery, Queenstown

BOTANICALS:
Juniper, Coriander Seed, Angelica Root, Cassia, Liquorice Extract, Orris Root, Cardamom, Chamomile, Lavender, Hypericum, Rosehip, Astragalus, Elderflower & Others

---

TASTING NOTES:
Floral elderflower, almond and rosehip on the nose with bright citrus and piney juniper on the palate. Herbacious finish.

SERVING SUGGESTION:
Enjoy with Fever-Tree Elderflower Tonic Water and a slice of lemon.

AWARDS:
NZ Spirits Awards — Silver 2019 & 2021

NEW ZEALAND
LIMITED EDITION
EST. 06
HAND CRAFTED
LIGHTHOUSE
BATCH DISTILLED
GIN
HAWTHORN EDITION
DISTILLED AND BOTTLED
IN NEW ZEALAND
57% ALC VOL. 700 ML
HERRICK CREEK
DISTILLERY
NINE FATHOMS
CANTERBURY GIN
Made from Canterbury Grains | Distilled with Nine Botanicals
Small Batch | Non-Chill Filtered
45°44'11.1"S 166°53'10.8"E
Christchurch   New Zealand

NAVY STRENGTH

NAVY STRENGTH GIN

The baseline for Navy Strength gin was traditionally the same style as London Dry but proofed at the higher ABV of 54.5% and above. Can be made in a Classic or Contemporary style.

Broken Heart Navy Strength Gin

57% ABV

A classic navy gin with a potency of 57%, Broken Heart Navy Strength Gin is based on their original Gin but with a stronger botanical flavour and impact.

GUIDE TO NEW ZEALAND GIN
— 2020 —
TASTERS' PICK

DISTILLERY:
Broken Heart Spirits,
Arrow Junction

BOTANICALS:
Juniper, Coriander, Citrus,
Angelica, Lavender, Orange
Flower, Hops, Ginger, Pimento
& Cinnamon

TASTING NOTES:
Dry and herbaceous green nose
with lots of lemon myrtle and
heat on the palate.
Clean finish.

SERVING SUGGESTION:
Enjoy with Fever-Tree
Mediterranean Tonic Water and
a slice of lemon.

Nine Fathoms Canterbury Gin

57% ABV

A contemporary navy gin with a potency of 57%, Nine Fathoms Canterbury Gin is named for and made in the spirit of a small passage between the mainland and Cooper Island in Fiordland where moose are said to have been spotted.

DISTILLERY:
Herrick Creek Distillery,
Christchurch

BOTANICALS:
Juniper, Coriander Seed, Angelica Root, Hops, Orange, Lemon, Cucumber, Horopito & Kiwifruit

---

TASTING NOTES:
Complex sweet citrusy nose with lots of pepper, citrus, bitter hops and tart fruit on the palate. Dryness and heat from the horopito on the finish.

SERVING SUGGESTION:
Enjoy with Fever-Tree Premium Indian Tonic Water and a slice of cucumber.

AWARDS:
NZ Spirits Awards – Bronze 2021

Island Gin Navy Strength

57% ABV

A contemporary navy strength gin with a potency of 57%, Isalnd Gin Navy Strength is nicknamed "Shark Alley" because it is "not for the faint of heart".

DISTILLERY:
Island Gin Distillery,
Great Barrier

BOTANICALS:
Juniper, Manuka Honey, Bush
Honey, Coriander Seed, Lemon
Myrtle & Others

TASTING NOTES:
Herbaceous and dry juniper on
the nose, coriander is earthy with
additional bush pepper, green
leaf and sweet herbs on the palate
before a very dry finish.

SERVING SUGGESTION:
Enjoy with Fever-Tree
Mediterranean Tonic Water
and a slice of lemon.

AWARDS:
NZ Spirits Award – Silver 2020
and IWSC – Silver 2021

Lighthouse Gin Hawthorn Edition

57% ABV

A classic navy gin with a potency of 57%, Lighthouse Gin Hawthorn Edition is inspired by a Wellington institution, the Hawthorn Lounge, an intimate speakeasy with a focus on cocktails.

DISTILLERY:
Lighthouse Gin Distillery, Martinborough

BOTANICALS:
Juniper, Coriander Seed, Yen Ben Lemon Zest, Navel Orange Zest, Cinnamon, Almond, Cassia Bark, Orris Root & Liquorice Root

TASTING NOTES:
Juniper, coriander, almond and roots on the nose, slightly creamy lemon on the palate with baking spice lingering from palate to finish.

SERVING SUGGESTION:
Enjoy with Fever-Tree Premium Indian Tonic Water and a slice of orange.

III

Old Navy - Navy Strength Gin

58% ABV

A contemporary navy gin with a potency of 58%, NDC's Old Navy – Navy Strength Gin is inspired by a classic London Dry gin with a tip of the hat to the pirates of old.

DISTILLERY:
The National Distillery Co., Napier

BOTANICALS:
Juniper, Coriander Seed, Angelica Root, Cardamom, Orris Root, Cassia Bark, Lemon Peel, Flax Seed & Liquorice Root

TASTING NOTES:
Peppery and hot on the nose opening to a softly spiced palate with citrus, spice and a touch of mentholic, astringency on the finish.

SERVING SUGGESTION:
Enjoy with Fever-Tree Aromatic Tonic Water and a slice of lemon.

AWARDS:
The Junipers – Silver 2020, NZ Spirits Awards – Bronze 2021, SIP Awards – Gold 2021, and San Francisco World Spirit Competition – Double Gold 2021

Roots Norwester Navy Strength Dry Gin

54.5% ABV

A contemporary navy gin with a potency of 54.5%, Roots Norwester Navy Strength Gin is a stronger bottling of their Marlborough Dry Gin with the addition of giant kelp from Akaroa and hemp seed from the Hawke's Bay.

DISTILLERY:
Elemental Distillers, Marlborough

BOTANICALS:
Juniper, Coriander, Grapefruit, Hops, Kawakawa Berry, Gorse Flower, Hemp Seed & Giant Kelp

TASTING NOTES:
Grassy nose with plenty of hops, natives and citrus. Kawakawa pepper and grapefruit on the palate with lingering bitterness on the long finish.

SERVING SUGGESTION:
Enjoy with Fever-Tree Mediterranean Tonic Water and a slice of grapefruit.

AWARDS:
NZ Spirits Awards – Silver 2021

SCAPEGRACE

NEW ZEALAND DISTILLING CO

Scapegrace Gold

57% ABV

A classic navy gin with a potency of 57%, Scapegrace Gold is a London Dry Gin made with the same 12 botanicals as their Classic gin with the addition of tangerine as a third layer of citrus.

DISTILLERY:

Scapegrace Distilling Co., Christchurch

BOTANICALS:

Juniper, Coriander Seed, Lemon Peel, Orange Peel, Cardamom, Nutmeg, Angelica Root, Liquorice Root, Orris Root, Clove, Cinnamon, Cassia Bark & Tangerine

TASTING NOTES:

Lemon and juniper on the nose, some sweetness and spice on the palate with hints of coriander and clove on the finish.

SERVING SUGGESTION:

Enjoy with Fever-Tree Premium Indian Tonic Water and a slice of orange.

AWARDS:

IWSC – Trophy Winner: World's Best London Dry 2018, and San Francisco World Spirits Competition – Gold 2016 & 2017, Double Gold 2018

1919 DISTILLING
DRY PINK
GIN
Est. 2017
HAND-CRAFTED SMALL BATCH
700ml
NEW ZEALAND MADE, DISTILLED & BOTTLED
ALC BY VOL 41%
82 PROOF
CONCEPT
BESPOKE DISTILLING
GIN
750ML

 PINK

PINK

A classic London Dry or Modern Dry gin that has natural pink colouring due to the redistillation of berries, red fruits or pink botanicals.

———————

1919 Pink Gin

41% ABV

A pink gin, the 1919 Pink Gin is distilled using raspberries and Auckland grown strawberries to capture the taste of summer and impart a pale pink colour.

DISTILLERY:
1919 Distilling, Auckland

BOTANICALS:
Juniper, Coriander Seed, Green Cardamom, Lemon Peel, Orange Peel, Angelica Root, Cherry, Manuka Honey, Cinnamon, Strawberries & Raspberries

---

TASTING NOTES:
Delicate berry nose, with berries, tart cherry, cardamom and coriander on the palate. A long citrus finish.

SERVING SUGGESTION:
Enjoy with Fever-Tree Mediterranean Tonic Water and fresh strawberries.

AWARDS:
New Zealand Artisan Awards — Alcohol Category Winner 2019, New Zealand Spirits Award — Bronze 2020 and Silver 2021 and Sip Awards — Platinum 2020 & Innovation Award 2020

batch10 Pink Gin

40% ABV

A pink gin, batch10 Pink Gin honours the historic recipe by balancing the light spice of bitters with the freshness of pomegranate in combination with their New Zealand Gin giving it a vibrant pink colour.

DISTILLERY:
batch10 Spirits, Puhoi

BOTANICALS:
Juniper, Coriander Seed, Cassia Bark, Angelica Root, Nutmeg, Citrus Peel, Tangerine, Orris Root, Star Anise, Anise, Lemon, Orange, Cardamom, Pomegranate & Bitters

---

TASTING NOTES:
Spice and fruit on the nose with a syrupy pomegranate, anise and nutmeg on the palate.
A dry finish.

SERVING SUGGESTION:
Enjoy with Fever-Tree Mediterranean Tonic Water and pomegranate seeds.

GUIDE TO NEW ZEALAND GIN

Concept Bespoke Distilling Pink Gin

40% ABV

A pink gin, Concept Bespoke Distilling's Pink Gin is made using NZ sourced flower petals and botanicals including hibiscus and rosehip which impart a deep, almost red, pink colour.

DISTILLERY:
Concept Brewing and Distilling, Christchurch

BOTANICALS:
Juniper, Wormwood, Hibiscus Petals & Rosehip

TASTING NOTES:
Raspberry leaf, black tea and earthy rhubarb on the nose with a dry and tart palate. A bitter and fast finish.

SERVING SUGGESTION:
Enjoy with Fever-Tree Elderflower Tonic Water and fresh raspberries.

Pink & White - Pink Dry

45% ABV

A pink gin, Pink & White's Pink Dry Gin combines blueberries, strawberries, and raspberries amongst other botanicals which impart it with a pale pink colour.

DISTILLERY:
Pink & White - Geothermal Gin, Rotorua

BOTANICALS:
Juniper, Clove, Blueberry, Strawberry, Raspberry & Others

TASTING NOTES:
Strawberries and cream on the nose with lots of anise, clove and cinnamon on the palate before a medium finish.

SERVING SUGGESTION:
Enjoy with Fever-Tree Mediterranean Tonic Water and fresh raspberries.

AWARDS:
NZ Spirits Awards — Silver 2021

CURIOSITY GIN
GIN
CURIOSITY
imagination
2021
DAMSON PLUM
& BLACKBERRY
NEW ZEALAND GIN LIQUEUR
ABV 32% | 700ml
No 05
QUINCE
GIN
BROKEN HEART
QUINCE
GIN
30% ALC BY VOL.
500ML
No 05 Eternal Optimist
BOTTLE No 205

FLAVOURED

FLAVOURED GIN

Made using compound methods or vacuum distillation to infuse or macerate flavour into gin.

SLOE GIN

A gin-based liqueur sweetened with sugar and flavoured by infusing sloe berries.

GIN LIQUEUR

A gin liqueur may be infused or macerated with additional flavours, including the addition of sugar and typically bottled at a lower ABV.

1919 Pineapple Bits Gin

41% ABV

A flavoured gin, 1919 Pineapple Bits Gin is all about classic Kiwiana with its taste of pineapple and chocolate and pale yellow colour.

DISTILLERY:
1919 Distilling, Auckland

BOTANICALS:
Juniper, Coriander Seed, Lemon Peel, Orange Peel, Angelica Root, Pineapple & Cacao Nibs

TASTING NOTES:
Pineapple and lemon on the nose with orange and cacao on the palate and a touch of coriander and root spice on the finish

SERVING SUGGESTION:
Enjoy with Fever-Tree Refreshingly Light Indian Tonic Water and a pineapple lolly.

AWARDS:
The Junipers New Zealand Gin Awards — Gold 2020

Blush Boysenberry Gin

37.5% ABV

A flavoured gin, Blush Boysenberry Gin is the world's first boysenberry gin, sourcing its star ingredient fresh from Nelson and imparting a bold dark red colour.

DISTILLERY:
Blush Gin Ltd., Auckland

BOTANICALS:
Juniper, Boysenberry, Citrus Peel, Anise, Cardamom & Angelica Root

TASTING NOTES:
Sweet raspberry and anise syrup on the nose with plenty of berry and sweet spice on the palate. Sweet finish.

SERVING SUGGESTION:
Enjoy with Fever-Tree Lemon Tonic Water and fresh boysenberries.

AWARDS:
Australian Gin Awards – Silver 2019 and NZ Spirits Awards – Bronze 2021

Blush Rhubarb Gin

37.5% ABV

A flavoured gin, the very first batch of Blush Rhubarb Gin was actually made in a 500ml jam jar and has a deep pink colour.

DISTILLERY:
Blush Gin Ltd., Auckland

BOTANICALS:
Juniper, Rhubarb, Liquorice Root, Coriander Seed, Cassia Bark, Angelica Root, Nutmeg, Citrus Peel, Tangerine, Orris Root & Star Anise

TASTING NOTES:
Rhubarb and root spice on the nose, with sweet rhubarb and spice on the palate. Sweet finish.

SERVING SUGGESTION:
Enjoy with Fever-Tree Elderflower Tonic Water and a sprig of mint.

AWARDS:
The Gin Is In Awards – Silver 2018 and NZ Spirits Awards – Bronze 2021

Blush Hot Toddy Gin

37.5% ABV

A flavoured gin, Blush Hot Toddy Gin is a tweaked version of their Rhubarb Gin with added fruits and spices associated with Christmas and the winter season giving it a warm amber colour.

DISTILLERY:

Blush Gin Ltd., Auckland

BOTANICALS:

Juniper, Cinnamon, Cardamom, Clove, Nutmeg, Apple, Raisin, Orris Root, Coriander Seed & Rhubarb

---

TASTING NOTES:

Christmas cake fruit and spice on the nose with clove, pepper, sweet cherry and raspberry on the palate with a touch of marzipan sugar. A long, sweet finish.

SERVING SUGGESTION:

Enjoy with Fever-Tree Aromatic Tonic Water and a slice of orange.

Blush Summer Citrus Gin

41.08% ABV

A flavoured gin, Blush Summer Citrus Gin is infused with citrus from sunny Kerikeri and rhubarb which give it a cloudy pale pink colour

DISTILLERY:
Blush Gin Ltd., Auckland

BOTANICALS:
Juniper, Rhubarb, Liquorice Root, Coriander Seed, Cassia Bark, Angelica Root, Nutmeg, Citrus Peel, Navel Orange, Lemon, Tangerine, Orris Root & Star Anise

---

TASTING NOTES:
Citrus essence and candied oranges on the nose with marmalade peel on the palate before a dry, hot finish.

SERVING SUGGESTION:
Enjoy with Fever-Tree Italian Blood Orange Soda and a slice of orange.

AWARDS:
NZ Spirits Awards — Bronze 2021

Broken Heart Pinot Noir Gin
40% ABV

A flavoured gin, Broken Heart Pinot Noir Gin is cold-soaked in Central Otago pinot noir grapes, creating a soft and sweet spirit with an autumn red colour.

DISTILLERY:
Broken Heart Spirits,
Arrow Junction

BOTANICALS:
Juniper, Coriander, Citrus, Angelica, Lavender, Orange Flower, Hops, Ginger, Pimento, Cinnamon & Pinot Noir Grapes

TASTING NOTES:
Fig and sultana on the nose with crisp buttery pastry before a sweet, dried fruit palate with a dry and tannic finish.

SERVING SUGGESTION:
Enjoy with Fever-Tree Lemon Tonic Water.

AWARDS:
NZ Spirits Awards —
Silver 2020

Broken Heart Quince Gin

30% ABV

A flavoured gin, Broken Heart Quince Gin is cold-soaked in organic quince, a fruit often symbolically associated with love, and has a rich amber colour.

DISTILLERY:
Broken Heart Spirits, Arrow Junction

BOTANICALS:
Juniper, Coriander, Citrus, Angelica, Lavender, Orange Flower, Hops, Ginger, Pimento, Cinnamon & Quince

TASTING NOTES:
Quince and juniper on the nose with tart quince and coriander on the palate with a herbaceous finish.

SERVING SUGGESTION:
Enjoy with Fever-Tree Mediterranean Tonic and a slice of orange.

AWARDS:
NZ Spirits Awards — Silver 2020

Broken Heart Rhubarb Gin

40% ABV

A flavoured gin, Broken Heart Rhubarb Gin is infused with a combination of organic green, pink, and red rhubarb resulting in a peachy pink colour.

DISTILLERY:
Broken Heart Spirits,
Arrow Junction

BOTANICALS:
Juniper, Coriander, Citrus,
Angelica, Lavender, Orange
Flower, Hop, Ginger, Pimento,
Cinnamon & Rhubarb

TASTING NOTES:
Earthy rhubarb and floral notes
on the nose with soft baking spice
and roots on the palate before a
bitter juniper finish.

SERVING SUGGESTION:
Enjoy with Fever-Tree Ginger Ale
and a slice orange.

Bureaucrats: Black Doris Plum

38% ABV

A flavoured gin, Bureaucrats: Black Doris Plum includes a combination of black doris plums and spices resulting in a delicate purple hue.

DISTILLERY:
Bureaucrats Gin Ltd., Wellington

BOTANICALS:
Juniper, Coriander Seed, Plum & Others

TASTING NOTES:
Earthy and delicate nose with some spice opens into a tart plum palate with coriander and a dry finish.

SERVING SUGGESTION:
Enjoy with Fever-Tree Ginger Ale and a cinnamon quill.

AWARDS:
NZ Spirits Awards — Bronze 2020

Concept Bespoke Distilling Blood Orange Gin

40% ABV

A flavoured gin, Concept Bespoke Distilling's Blood Orange Gin is made using raspberry, blood orange, and NZ sourced flower petals among other botanicals giving it a vibrant blood red colour.

DISTILLERY:

Concept Brewing and Distilling, Christchurch

BOTANICALS:

Juniper, Cardamom, Coriander, Liquorice Root, Angelica, Citrus Peel, Apple, Raspberry, Blood Orange, Hibiscus & Rosehip

---

TASTING NOTES:

Earthy, dried fruit nose with tart baking apples and bitter orange. Lots of spice on the palate and a dry finish.

SERVING SUGGESTION:

Enjoy with Fever-Tree Italian Blood Orange Soda and a slice of orange.

Concept Bespoke Distilling Blueberry Gin

40% ABV

A flavoured gin, Concept Bespoke Distilling's Blueberry Gin is fruited with real blueberries sourced in New Zealand that give it an inky purple red colour.

DISTILLERY:
Concept Brewing and Distilling,
Christchurch

BOTANICALS:
Juniper, Blueberry, Cornflower,
Chamomile, Cardamom,
Coriander, Liquorice Root
& Angelica

TASTING NOTES:
Earthy dried blueberries and chamomile on the nose with caramelised sugar and tea on the palate, somewhat astringent and tart finish.

SERVING SUGGESTION:
Enjoy with Fever-Tree Elderflower Tonic Water and fresh blueberries.

Curiosity Gin - Ruby

37.5% ABV

A flavoured gin, Curiosity Gin - Ruby is made by infusing their Curious Dry Gin with fresh Otaki rhubarb stalks and a little added sweetness resulting in a delicate cloudy red hue.

DISTILLERY:
The Spirits Workshop Distillery,
Christchurch

BOTANICALS:
Juniper, Tarata, Kawakawa,
Horopito, Manuka
& Rhubarb

TASTING NOTES:
Candy-sweet rhubarb and earthy
tarata on the nose with punchy
sweetness and horopito pepper
on the palate with a chewy finish.

SERVING SUGGESTION:
Enjoy with Fever-Tree Lemon
Tonic Water and a slice
of lemon.

AWARDS:
NZ Spirits Awards – Silver 2020
& Bronze 2021

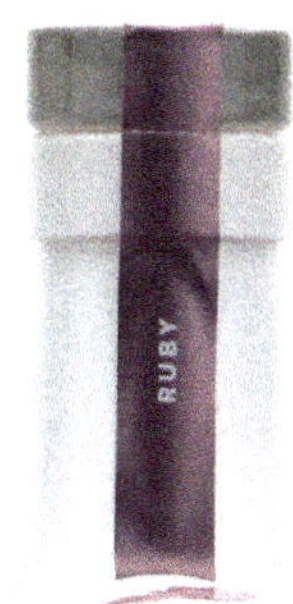

Curiosity Gin - Pinot Barrel Sloe

27% ABV

A sloe gin, Curiosity Gin Pinot Barrel Sloe is made the traditional way by steeping sloe berries in their Curious Dry gin in barrels previously used to age Otago Pinot Noir for several months.

DISTILLERY:
The Spirits Workshop Distillery, Christchurch

BOTANICALS:
Juniper, Manuka Berries & Leaves, Coriander Seed, Cardamom, Orange Zest, Angelica Root, Lavender, Cinnamon, Star Anise & Sloe Berries

TASTING NOTES:
Sloe berry and tannins from pinot noir on the nose. Sweet and smooth on the palate with soft baking spice before a light, quick finish.

SERVING SUGGESTION:
Enjoy with Fever-Tree Lemon Tonic Water and a slice of lemon.

AWARDS:
NZ Spirits Awards – Silver 2020 & 2021

Dancing Sands Sauvignon Blanc Gin

37.5% ABV

A flavoured gin, Dancing Sands Sauvignon Blanc Gin is made using a vacuum distillation process that infuses New Zealand sauvignon blanc wine with their Dry Gin while preserving the wine's original flavor.

DISTILLERY:
Dancing Sands Distillery, Takaka

BOTANICALS:
Juniper, Coriander Seed, Angelica Root, Manuka, Cardamom, Peppercorn, Almond, Liquorice Root & Sauvignon Blanc Wine

TASTING NOTES:
Astringent sauvignon blanc and lime on the nose with fresh, green herbaceousness. Sweet and tangy on the palate with a green spice and peppery finish.

SERVING SUGGESTION:
Enjoy with Fever-Tree Refreshingly Light Tonic Water and a slice of lime.

AWARDS:
NZ Spirits Awards – Silver 2021

Dancing Sands Sun-Kissed Gin

37.5% ABV

A flavoured gin, Dancing Sands Sun-Kissed Gin is made using fresh strawberries and locally sourced rhubarb which are then candied before infusion giving it a pale pink colour.

DISTILLERY:

Dancing Sands Distillery, Takaka

BOTANICALS:

Juniper, Coriander Seed, Angelica Root, Manuka, Cardamom, Peppercorn, Almond, Liquorice Root, Strawberry & Rhubarb

---

TASTING NOTES:

Sweet baking spice and fruit on the nose with lots of sweetness, green spice and pepper on the palate. A sweet finish.

SERVING SUGGESTION:

Enjoy with Fever-Tree Lemon Tonic Water and fresh strawberries.

AWARDS:

SIP Awards – Silver 2019, NZ Spirits Awards – Silver 2019, and San Francisco World Spirit Awards – Bronze Medal 2019

Good George Day Off Doris Plum Gin

45% ABV

A flavoured gin, Good George Day Off Doris Plum Gin is a spin on their original Day Off Gin with an infusion of doris plums and pink peppercorns which impart a rich red colour.

DISTILLERY:
Good George Distillery,
Hamilton

BOTANICALS:
Juniper, Coriander Seed,
Angelica Root, Liquorice Root,
Pink Peppercorn, Rosehip,
Cardamom, Star Anise, Bitter
Orange Peel, Chamomile, Doris
Plum & Hibiscus

TASTING NOTES:
Sweet plum nose with hints
of juniper and coriander.
Cardamom and green spice on
the palate with touches of rose and
hibiscus, a dry tea finish.

SERVING SUGGESTION:
Enjoy with Fever-Tree Lemon
Tonic Water and a slice of orange.

AWARDS:
NZ Spirits Awards – Bronze 2021

Good George Day Off Feijoa Gin

45% ABV

A flavoured gin, Good George Day Off Feijoa Gin draws on their experience of adding a feijoa spin to their other products by adding 40kg of them to the still after distillation.

DISTILLERY:
Good George Distillery, Hamilton

BOTANICALS:
Juniper, Coriander Seed, Angelica Root, Rosehip, Liquorice Root, Pink Peppercorn, Feijoa, Cardamom, Lime & Star Anise

TASTING NOTES:
Soft feijoa and star anise on the nose with lots of coriander and cardamom on the palate, a slightly bitter dry finish.

SERVING SUGGESTION:
Enjoy with Fever-Tree Refreshingly Light Indian Tonic Water and a fresh feijoa.

AWARDS:
NZ Spirits Awards – Silver 2020 and London Spirits Competition – Bronze 2020

Damson Plum & Blackberry Gin Liqueur
32% ABV

A gin liqueur, imagination's Damson Plum & Blackberry Gin Liqueur is inspired by an old English recipe that highlights New Zealand's seasonal autumn produce including plums that were macerated in their dry gin for four months giving it a deep purple red colour.

DISTILLERY:
imagination, Reikorangi

BOTANICALS:
Juniper, Coriander Seed, Cinnamon, Liquorice Root, Orris Root, Orange, Lime, Lemon, Manuka, Damon Plums & Blackberries

TASTING NOTES:
Soft baking spice with cinnamon, orris root and liquorice root on the nose, tart, juicy plum and berry on the palate with citrus peel on the finish.

SERVING SUGGESTION:
Enjoy with Fever-Tree Lemon Tonic Water and a slice of lemon.

AWARDS:
NZ Spirits Awards – Bronze 2020

Reikorangi Rhubarb & Raspberry Gin

38% ABV

A flavoured gin, Reikorangi Rhubarb & Raspberry Gin is inspired by
the New Zealand summer using raspberries macerated in a floral dry gin
and blended with slowly extracted rhubarb juice which gives it a bold pink
red colour.

DISTILLERY:
imagination, Reikorangi

BOTANICALS:
Juniper, Coriander Seed,
Angelica Root, Manuka,
Cardamom, Peppercorn, Almond
& Liquorice Root

TASTING NOTES:
Raspberry, vanilla and rhubarb
on the nose with a warming spice
and liquorice on the palate.
Very dry finish.

SERVING SUGGESTION:
Enjoy with Fever-Tree
Refreshingly Light Indian Tonic
Water and fresh raspberries.

AWARDS:
NZ Spirits Awards – Silver 2020

Lavender Infused Gin

40% ABV

A flavoured gin, Lavender Infused Gin is made using the essential oils from their own commercial fields of 'Pacific Blue' English lavender (Angustifolia) which is hand harvested and extracted on the farm.

DISTILLERY:
Lavender Hill, Riverhead

BOTANICALS:
Juniper, Coriander Seed, Cassia Bark, Angelica Root, Nutmeg, Citrus Peel, Tangerine, Orris Root, Star Anise, Anise, Lemon, Orange, Cardamom & Lavandula Angustifolia

---

TASTING NOTES:
Soft and floral nose with hints of lavendar. Sweetness and spiced orange fruits on the palate with a slightly nutty and dry finish.

SERVING SUGGESTION:
Enjoy with Fever-Tree Elderflower Tonic Water and a slice of lemon.

AWARDS:
NZ Spirits Awards – Silver 2020

Saffron Infused Gin

40% ABV

A flavoured gin, Saffron Infused Gin is made using 100% organic saffron from a partner farm in the South Island producing a vibrant yellow colour.

DISTILLERY:
Lavender Hill, Riverhead

BOTANICALS:
Juniper, Coriander Seed, Cassia Bark, Angelica Root, Nutmeg, Citrus Peel, Tangerine, Orris Root, Star Anise, Anise, Lemon, Orange, Cardamom & Saffron

---

TASTING NOTES:
A soft piney nose with a rush of saffron and coriander on the palate before a soft, dry finish.

SERVING SUGGESTION:
Enjoy with Fever-Tree Refreshingly Light Tonic Water and a slice of orange.

AWARDS:
NZ Spirits Awards
— Bronze 2020

Rose & Twig Blood Orange Gin

37.5% ABV

A flavoured gin, Rose & Twig Blood Orange Gin is triple distilled with 6 botanicals including ripe blood oranges which impart it with a vibrant red-tinged orange colour.

DISTILLERY:

Premium Liquor Co., Auckland

BOTANICALS:

Juniper, Coriander Seed, Orris Root, Angelica Root, Citrus Peel & Blood Orange

TASTING NOTES:

Sweet orange and bitter pith on the nose, slightly astringent with heavy cardamom and baking spice on the palate.
A sweet finish.

SERVING SUGGESTION:

Enjoy with Fever-Tree Refreshingly Light Indian Tonic Water and a slice of blood orange.

GUIDE TO NEW ZEALAND GIN

Rose & Twig Blueberry Gin

37.5% ABV

A flavoured gin, Rose & Twig Blueberry Gin is triple distilled with 6 botanicals including blueberries which give it a rich indigo colour.

DISTILLERY:
Premium Liquor Co., Auckland

BOTANICALS:
Juniper, Coriander Seed, Orris Root, Angelica Root, Citrus Peel & Blueberry

---

TASTING NOTES:
Blueberry extract and pepper on the nose with astringent berry and sweetness on the palate. A touch of root spice on the dry finish.

SERVING SUGGESTION:
Enjoy with Fever-Tree Lemon Tonic Water and fresh blueberries.

Rose & Twig Pomegranate

37.5% ABV

A flavoured gin, Rose & Twig Pomegranate Gin is triple distilled with 6 botanicals and infused with pomegranate juice which imparts a delicate pink colour.

DISTILLERY:
Premium Liquor Co., Auckland

BOTANICALS:
Juniper, Coriander Seed, Orris Root, Angelica Root, Citrus Peel & Pomegranate

TASTING NOTES:
Caramelised orange peel and black pepper on the nose with red fruit and peppery spice on the palate before a hot, dry finish.

SERVING SUGGESTION:
Enjoy with Fever-Tree Lemon Tonic Water and pomegranate seeds.

Solace Cranberry & Raspberry Gin
37.5% ABV

A flavoured gin, Solace Cranberry & Raspberry Gin uses their Dry Gin as a base and is then sweetened with natural berry extracts which also give it a deep pink colour.

DISTILLERY:
Kings Liquor, Auckland

BOTANICALS:
Juniper, Coriander Seed, Cassia Bark, Angelica Root, Nutmeg, Citrus Peel, Tangerine, Orris Root, Star Anise, Anise, Lemon, Orange, Cardamom & Natural Berry Extract

---

TASTING NOTES:
Herbacious sweet candied lemon on the nose with anise, liquorice and mixed berry fruit on the palate before a soft, spiced finish.

SERVING SUGGESTION:
Enjoy with Fever-Tree Lemon Tonic Water and fresh raspberries.

Takapuna Berry Pink Gin

40% ABV

A flavoured gin, Takapuna Berry Pink Gin includes raspberry, strawberry, and rhubarb amongst its botanicals which impart it with an ephemeral pink colour.

DISTILLERY:
CarbonSix Distillery, Auckland

BOTANICALS:
Juniper, Raspberry, Strawberry, Rhubarb & Others

TASTING NOTES:
Resin and vegetal notes on the nose with some berry sweetness and bush pepper on the palate, lots of coriander in the dry finish.

SERVING SUGGESTION:
Enjoy with Fever-Tree Lemon Tonic Water and fresh raspberries.

Takapuna Cheese Cake Gin
40% ABV

A flavoured gin, Takapuna Cheese Cake Gin riffs on the idea of making cheesecakes with gin by doing the reverse and making a gin using cheesecake as an ingredient.

DISTILLERY:
CarbonSix Distillery, Auckland

————————————

BOTANICALS:
Juniper & Others

————————————

TASTING NOTES:
Spirit forward nose with lots of pepper, vanilla and caramel hints. A touch of vanilla sweetness on the palate before a hot, dry finish.

————————————

SERVING SUGGESTION:
Enjoy with Fever-Tree Refreshingly Light Tonic Water and fresh strawberries.

Takapuna Manuka Honey Gin

40% ABV

A flavoured gin, Takapuna Manuka Honey Gin's signature botanical is of course manuka honey, famed for its sweet and creamy texture, which gives it a cloudy pale yellow colour.

DISTILLERY:
CarbonSix Distillery, Auckland

BOTANICALS:
Juniper, Lemon, Manuka Honey & Others

TASTING NOTES:
Lemony, rich nose with more sweet citrus on the palate and velvety sweetness on the palate. A creamy and lingering spice finish.

SERVING SUGGESTION:
Enjoy with Fever-Tree Lemon Tonic Water and a slice of lemon.

Takapuna Zesty Citrus Gin
40% ABV

A flavoured gin, Takapuna Zesty Citrus Gin is made using whole lemons, limes, and oranges in contrast to the traditional method of just using their peels.

DISTILLERY:
CarbonSix Distillery, Auckland

BOTANICALS:
Juniper, Lemon, Lime, Orange
& Others

TASTING NOTES:
Orange essence on the nose, spirit-forward with coriander and candied orange on the palate, bitter bark and orange on the finish.

SERVING SUGGESTION:
Enjoy with Fever-Tree Mediterranean Tonic Water and a slice of lemon.

AWARDS:
NZ Spirits Awards –
Bronze 2021

Victor Gin Blanc De Blancs

42% ABV

A flavoured gin, Victor Gin Blanc De Blancs is made by marrying the botanicals in their Original gin and chardonnay grape juice from their local region.

DISTILLERY:
Thomson Whisky Distillery,
Riverhead

————————

BOTANICALS:
Juniper, Lemon, Lemongrass,
Cardamom, Coriander & New
Zealand Chardonnay Grape Juice

————————

TASTING NOTES:
Candied lemongrass, lemon
sorbet and sweet grapes on the
nose, sweet lemon and coriander
on the palate with a slightly
sweet finish.

————————

SERVING SUGGESTION:
Enjoy over ice or with Fever-Tree
Premium Soda Water.

Waiheke Distilling Co. Ruby Red Gin

42% ABV

A flavoured gin, Waiheke Distilling Co.'s Ruby Red Gin is the 'jewel' in their collection infused with sweet New Zealand cherries and boasting a luscious red colour.

DISTILLERY:
Waiheke Distilling Co., Waiheke

BOTANICALS:
Juniper & Others

TASTING NOTES:
Sweet cherry, lime and clove on the nose with more baking spice on the palate before a resinous, oily finish.

SERVING SUGGESTION:
Enjoy with Fever-Tree Lemon Tonic Water and slice of lime.

AWARDS:
NZ Spirits Awards
– Silver 2021

Sheep Milk & Honey Gin

42% ABV

A flavoured gin, White Sheep Co.'s Sheep Milk & Honey Gin uses a fermented sheep's milk spirit and includes premium local honey among its botanicals which evokes the idea of New Zealand being a 'land of milk and honey' and imparts a golden hue.

DISTILLERY:

The White Sheep Co., Whangamata

BOTANICALS:

Juniper, Manuka Honey, Angelica Root, Orris Root, Clementine Zest, Coriander Seed, Lemon Zest & Allspice

---

TASTING NOTES:

Gentle spice, citrus and honey nose with creamed clover honey, root spice and pepper on the palate before a soft, velvety finish.

SERVING SUGGESTION:

Enjoy with Fever-Tree Refreshingly Light Indian Tonic Water.

AWARDS:

New Zealand Food Awards – Best Alcoholic Beverage 2019 and Innovation Award 2019, NZ Spirits Awards– Bronze 2020 and CWSA – Gold Medal 2020

Wild Diamond Feijoa Gin
42% ABV

A flavoured gin, Wild Diamond Feijoa Gin is a limited edition that uses their Rare Dry Gin as the base with an extra infusion of organic feijoa giving it a soft golden colour.

DISTILLERY:
Wild Diamond Distillery, Queenstown

BOTANICALS:
Juniper, Coriander Seed, Angelica Root, Cassia, Liquorice Extract, Orris Root, Cardamom, Chamomile, Lavender, Hypericum, Rosehip, Astragalus, Elderflower, Feijoa & Others

---

TASTING NOTES:
Slightly astringent feijoa, apple and citrus nose before a palate full of spice and spirit. A hot, dry finish.

SERVING SUGGESTION:
Enjoy with Fever-Tree Mediterranean Tonic Water and a fresh feijoa.

Wild Diamond Vanilla Gin

42% ABV

A flavoured gin, Wild Diamond Vanilla Gin is a limited edition that uses their Rare Dry Gin as the base with an extra infusion of organic vanilla giving it a pale golden colour.

DISTILLERY:

Wild Diamond Distillery, Queenstown

BOTANICALS:

Juniper, Coriander Seed, Angelica Root, Cassia, Liquorice Extract, Orris Root, Cardamom, Chamomile, Lavender, Hypericum, Rosehip, Astragalus, Elderflower, Vanilla & Others

---

TASTING NOTES:

Softer floral nose with hints of vanilla and cassia bark. Peppery on the palate with cinnamon and liquorice lingering on the finish.

SERVING SUGGESTION:

Enjoy with Fever-Tree Refreshingly Light Indian Tonic Water.

imagination
BB
B120
BLACK BARN SYRAH
BARREL AGED
NEW ZEALAND GIN
ABV 44.2% | 700ml

AGED

AGED GIN

An aged gin refers to any gin that has been finished
for any period of time with additional ingredients
or influence, including the addition of staves or
woodchip in tank or keg prior to bottling. The use of
wood components produces an aged effect and wood
influence on the gin.

BARREL/CASK AGED GIN

Matured in barrel or cask for ant period of time.

Awildian Coromandel Manuka Gin

47% ABV

An aged gin, Awildian Coromandel Manuka Gin is rested in toasted Manuka wood coated with medicinal grade Manuka Honey for no less than 3 months which imparts a pale golden colour.

DISTILLERY:

Coromandel Distilling Co., Thames

BOTANICALS:

Juniper, Coriander, Angelica, Grains of Paradise, Chamomile, Voatsiperifery, Cubeb, Ginger, Orange, Cinnamon, Vanilla, Manuka Honey, Lavender, Orris, Liquorice & Others

TASTING NOTES:

Green and fresh manuka, bush mint and menthol on the nose with sweet orange, ginger and pepper on the palate with a warm, woody finish.

SERVING SUGGESTION:

Enjoy with Fever-Tree Smoky Ginger Ale and a slice of orange.

AWARDS:

San Francisco World Spirits Competition – Silver Medal 2021, International Wine and Spirits Awards – Silver 2021 and Dish Magazine Tasting Panel – Top Pick 2021

Broken Heart Barrel Aged Gin

40% ABV

A barrel aged gin that spends a year in French chardonnay oak, Broken Heart Barrel Aged Gin is warm and welcoming with a delicate golden hue.

DISTILLERY:
Broken Heart Spirits,
Arrow Junction

BOTANICALS:
Juniper, Coriander, Citrus, Angelica, Lavender, Orange Flower, Hop, Ginger, Pimento & Cinnamon

---

TASTING NOTES:
Juniper, oak and coriander on the nose and a slightly sweet oaky palate with lavendar emerging on the finish.

SERVING SUGGESTION:
Enjoy neat, over ice, or with Fever-Tree Ginger Beer.

Curiosity Gin - Negroni Special

55% ABV

A barrel aged gin, Curiosity Gin - Negroni Special is rested in new French oak barrels and designed to complement a Negroni cocktail with a soft golden hue.

DISTILLERY:
The Spirits Workshop Distillery, Christchurch

BOTANICALS:
Juniper, Coriander Seed, Orange Zest, Lime Zest, Ginger Root, Angelica Root, Lavender, Cinnamon, Cardamom & Star Anise

---

TASTING NOTES:
Fennel and aniseed on the nose with rich orange zest and spices on the palate. A dry, bitter finish with ginger and fennel.

SERVING SUGGESTION:
Enjoy with Fever-Tree Refreshingly Light Clementine Tonic Water and a slice of orange.

AWARDS:
New York World Wine and Spirits Competition — Silver 2017, San Francisco World Spirits Competition Gold 2018, SIP Awards — Silver 2018, and NZ Spirits Awards — Silver 2019 & Gold 2020

The Pioneer

46% ABV

An aged gin, The Pioneer was made to reflect the efforts of the early European settlers that came to New Zealand by taking the barrel to the gin rather than the gin to the barrel.

DISTILLERY:

Fenton Street Distillery, Stratford

BOTANICALS:

Juniper, Kawakawa, Angelica, Coriander, Oak Wine Staves, Tarata, Horopito, Citrus, Pepper, Ginger, Cassia Bark, Nutmeg, Honey & Manuka

TASTING NOTES:

Spiced tannins, vanilla and bush honey on the nose, slightly sweet pepper and nutmeg on the palate with subtle citrus and a peppery, damp green finish.

SERVING SUGGESTION:

Enjoy with Fever-Tree Indian Tonic Water.

AWARDS:

The Junipers – Gold (Matured), and Best in Class (Matured) 2020

Black Barn Syrah Barrel Aged Gin

44.2% ABV

A barrel aged gin matured in lightly toasted French oak barrels, Black Barn Syrah Barrel Aged Gin is made with their highest quality triple distilled gin and has a dusky pink colour.

DISTILLERY:
imagination, Reikorangi

BOTANICALS:
Juniper, Coriander Seed, Cinnamon, Liquorice Root, Orris Root, Orange, Lime, Lemon & Manuka

TASTING NOTES:
Rich berries and tannins on the nose with earthy liquorice, orris root and spice on the palate before a long, dry and citrusy finish.

SERVING SUGGESTION:
Enjoy neat, over ice or with Fever-Tree Spiced Orange Ginger Ale.

AWARDS:
SIP Awards – Silver 2020, IWSC – Bronze 2020, and NZ Spirits Awards – Bronze 2020

Little Biddy Gin - Cask Aged (Bourbon)

47% ABV

A barrel aged gin rested in ex-Bourbon American oak casks for two and a half months, Little Biddy Gin — Cask Aged (Bourbon) is infused with 13 botanicals and is imparted with a golden amber colour.

DISTILLERY:

Reefton Distilling Co., Reefton

BOTANICALS:

Juniper, Horopito, Rimu, Tarata, Toatoa, Douglas Fir, Lemon Peel, Angelica, Cardamom, Cassia, Coriander, Liquorice & Orris Root

---

TASTING NOTES:

Sweet citrus and vanilla on the nose with liquorice and wood spice on the palate before a soft and gentle finish.

SERVING SUGGESTION:

Enjoy neat or over ice.

AWARDS:

The Junipers — Bronze 2020 and NZ Spirits Awards — Silver 2021

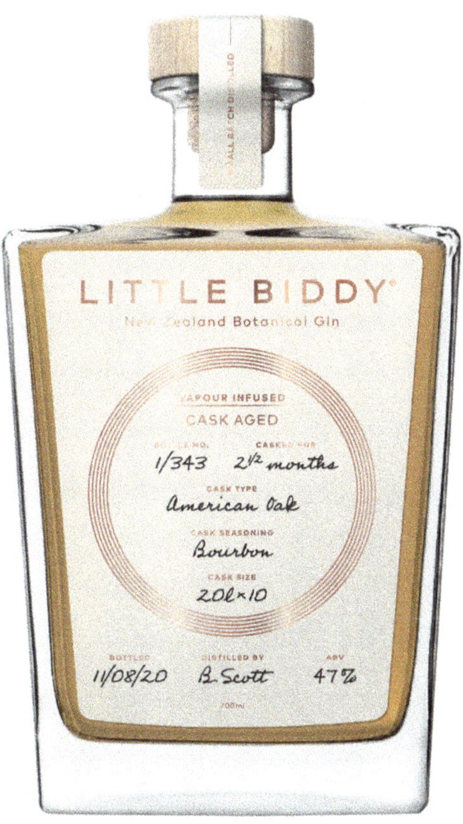

GUIDE TO NEW ZEALAND GIN

Reid + Reid Barrel Aged Gin

42% ABV

A barrel aged gin spending three months in ex-Martinborough pinot noir French oak barrels, Reid + Reid Barrel Aged Gin uses their Native Gin as its base and has a golden amber colour.

DISTILLERY:
Reid + Reid Distillery, Martinborough

BOTANICALS:
Juniper, Coriander Seed, Angelica Root, Liquorice Root, Orris Root, Fennel Seed, Nutmeg, Cassia, Cardamom, Orange Peel, Kawakawa, Horopito & Manuka

---

TASTING NOTES:
Slightly sweet and tannic nose with warm spice and cherry, kawakawa and pepper on the palate before lingering horopito on the finish.

SERVING SUGGESTION:
Enjoy neat, over ice or with Fever-Tree Ginger Beer.

ECOLOGY+CO
LONDON DRY
BOTANICAL BLEND
DISTILLED ALCOHOL-FREE SPIRITS
700ml · 0% ABV · NEW ZEALAND

ALCOHOL-FREE SPIRIT

ALCOHOL-FREE SPIRIT

Distilled without the presence of alcohol resulting in a
an alcohol-free distilled spirit.

———————————————

Ecology & Co. Asian Spice

ALCOHOL FREE SPIRIT

An alcohol free spirit, Ecology & Co. Asian Spice is made using a variety of herbs and spices from across Asia and elsewhere aimed at those with an adventurous or evolved palette.

DISTILLERY:
Ecology & Co., Auckland

BOTANICALS:
Cardamom, Black Pepper, Cassia, Basil, Cumin & Lemon Myrtle

TASTING NOTES:
Spice driven aromatics on the nose with a light and clean palate that carries cardamom through.

SERVING SUGGESTION:
Enjoy with Fever-Tree Refreshingly Light Indian Tonic Water and a slice of lemon.

Ecology & Co. London Dry

ALCOHOL FREE SPIRIT

An alcohol free spirit, Ecology & Co. London Dry focuses on a traditional blend of gin botanicals to create an alcohol-free replacement for the liquor in a G&T.

DISTILLERY:
Ecology & Co., Auckland

BOTANICALS:
Juniper, Coriander, Lemon, Liquorice Root, Angelica, Cassia, Basil, Cumin, Black Pepper & Orris

---

TASTING NOTES:
Citrus and bitter peel on the nose with a slightly bitter palate and astringent, powdery finish.

SERVING SUGGESTION:
Enjoy with Fever-Tree Refreshingly Light Indian Tonic Water and a slice of lemon.

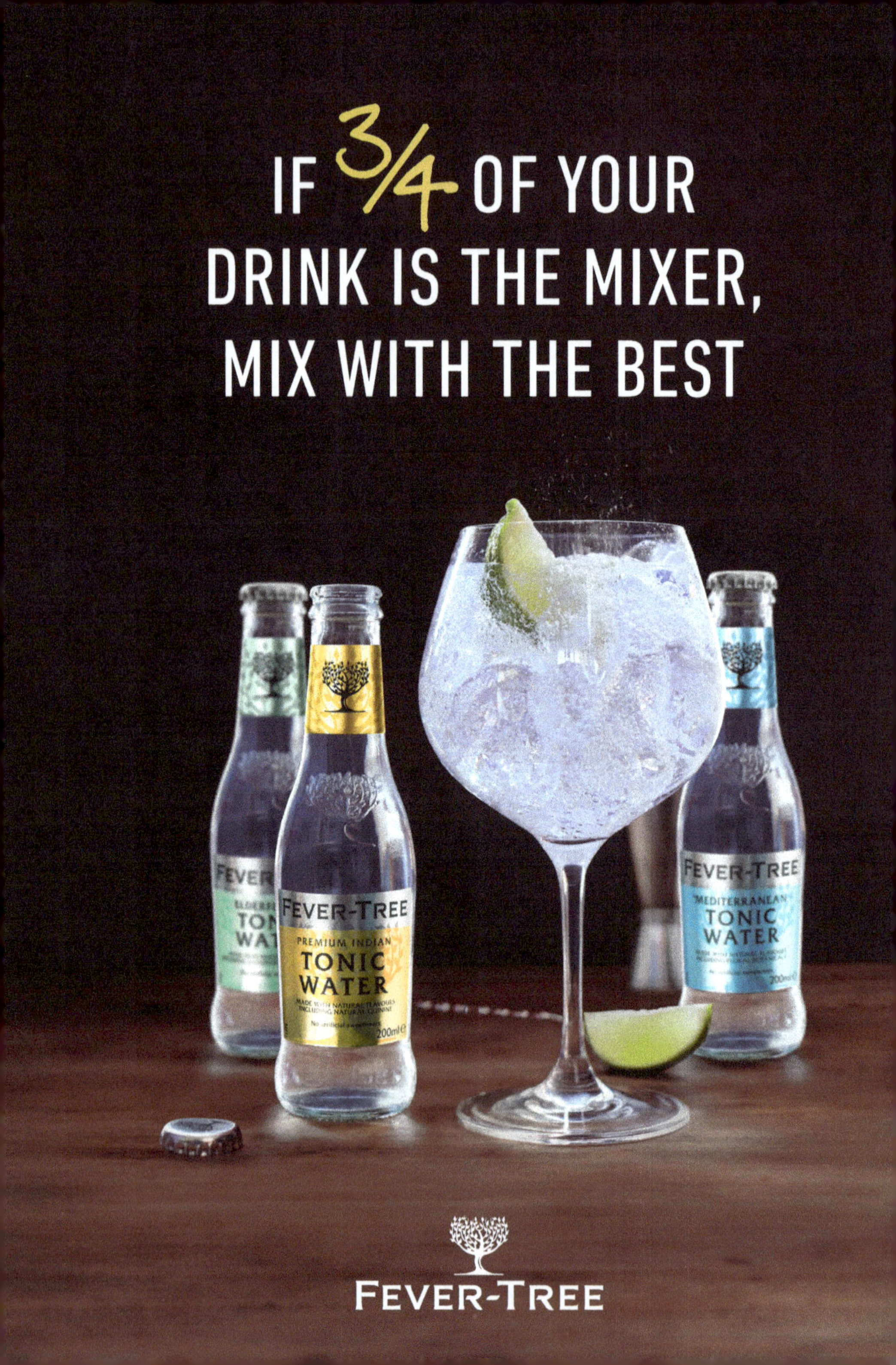
IF 3/4 OF YOUR
DRINK IS THE MIXER,
MIX WITH THE BEST
FEVER-TREE
PREMIUM INDIAN
TONIC WATER
200ml
FEVER-TREE
MEDITERRANEAN
TONIC WATER
FEVER-TREE

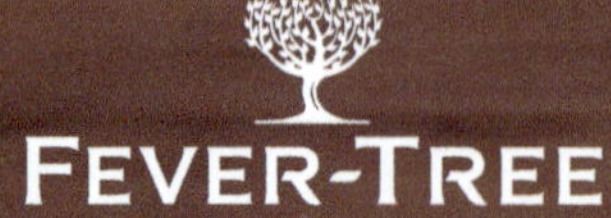

A SHORT HISTORY OF TONIC

NO CARBONATION, NO TONIC. NO TONIC, NO FEVER-TREE!
Does not bear thinking about. We have gin, we have ice and now we have
carbonation. But what about tonic?

To find the answer to that question you only have to look at the name itself.
You see, unlike gin, tonic really does have medicinal qualities to it. Or at least,
quinine which is found in the bark of the Cinchona Tree from which Tonic
is made does (and just as well too). In the 1600's, with the world plagued
by malaria carrying mosquitos, a Jesuit monk called Agostino (Jesuits were
considered the geniuses of the time) discovered that native Indians who would
chew the Cinchona bark when they had fever would see their fever subside.

So, he wondered whether it could do the same with Malaria – and hey presto!
The medicine was sent all over Europe and for the first time ever there was a
way to prevent the epidemic spreading.

In the 1800s, we saw the first 'Indian Tonic Waters' created as the British soldiers
stationed in India mixed their daily ration of quinine with 'a spoonful of sugar
to help the medicine go down' along with some local spices and citrus. That
little Cinchona bark pretty much changed the world. These enterprising soldiers
and their counter parts in the Royal Navy couldn't resist mixing this medicinal
mixture with their ration of gin. The humble G&T. This little concoction
revolutionised the way people took their daily medicine and also when they
took it. With the mosquitos choosing to come out as the sun went down, all
over Europe people would raise a glass at sunset and enjoy a gin and tonic as a
pleasantly social ritual.

In London, gin's reputation was on the rise. So much was gin's transformation
that it inspired one London-based gentleman, an Erasmus Bond, to come up
with the simple, yet wonderful idea of a pre-made tonic. In doing so, the social
status of the drink had now been well and truly elevated.

DID YOU KNOW?
Under a UV light, the quinine in tonic water makes the water fluoresce a
brilliant bright blue.

SIR WINSTON CHURCHILL SAID...
*"Gin and tonic has saved more Englishmen's lives, and minds, than all the
doctors in the Empire!"*

HOW TO CREATE THE PERFECT GIN & TONIC

It all began in 2003 with a meeting of minds and one simple premise: if three quarters of your G&T is the tonic, wouldn't you want it to be the best?

REIGNITING A LONG-FORGOTTEN AND NEGLECTED SECTOR OF THE DRINKS INDUSTRY

Our co-founders Charles and Tim, working in different parts of the drinks business, had both spotted that premium spirits were growing quickly, fuelled by consumers' increasing awareness of the provenance of what they ate and drank.

However, this growing interest in premium food and drink had seemed to neglect mixers, a crucial element of the drinks industry that remained flat. It struck them both as extraordinary that people were paying a good deal of money for a high-quality spirit, yet had no choice but drown it with a poor-quality mixer

CHARLES AND TIM SET OUT TO PUT QUALITY BACK INTO MIXERS

From the very beginning, Charles and Tim approached their business in a different way – there would be no compromise at Fever-Tree. Flavour and quality were of the utmost importance. This mindset led them on an 18-month adventure from the archives of the British Library to facing the wrong end of a Kalashnikov in the Democratic Republic of Congo and concluded with the launch of our Premium Indian Tonic Water in 2005, with the belief we still operate by today…

PIONEERING TO PRODUCE AN UNRIVALLED DRINKING EXPERIENCE AT EVERY OCCASION

Since we put the lid on our first bottle of our Premium Indian Tonic Water, we haven't wavered in our single-minded mission to bring quality, flavour and choice back to mixers. Innovation remains at the heart of Fever-Tree and we've developed an award winning range of tonic waters that perfectly complement the varied flavour categories of gin. We've found three incredibly diverse varieties of ginger that, together, create a remarkably deep, fresh and true taste, which we've used to make a selection of ginger ales and ginger beer. We have lemonades using the finest,

naturally sourced ingredients and have recently launched our Soda Collection – A brand-new range of three mouth-watering flavoured sodas, including Lime & Yuzu, Italian Blood Orange and Pink Grapefruit. Our story is about going to the ends of the earth in pursuit of the best and, the most exciting thing is, we've only just scratched the surface.

OUR MIXERS

We start with the idea that, if ¾ of your drink is the mixer, then you should use the best. We work with only the best naturally sourced ingredients from around the world and no artificial flavourings or sweeteners to create mixers that do justice to the world's finest spirits

PAIR YOUR FAVOURITE PREMIUM GINS WITH FEVER-TREE MIXERS

Gin is an often overlooked spirit, despite its incredibly rich diversity. Bursts of juicy citrus, deliciously savoury herb notes and crisp, floral flavours are just some of the immense range of characteristics this one spirit can contain. Fever-Tree has been on a relentless pioneering pursuit to create a selection of award-winning tonic waters, each one individually crafted to complement the diverse flavour profiles of gin. While made with gins in mind, our tonics pair equally as well.

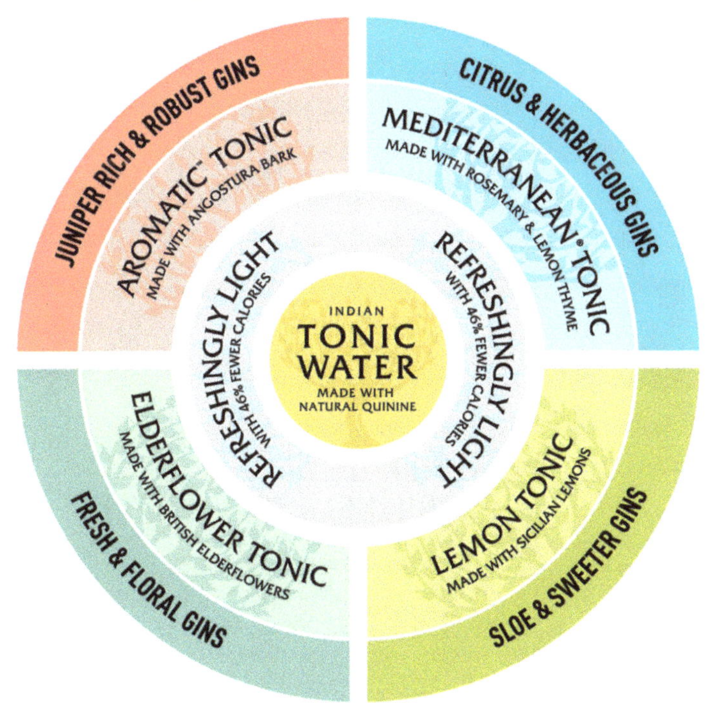

TONICS

PREMIUM INDIAN TONIC WATER

By blending luscious botanical oils with spring water and quinine of the highest quality from the 'fever trees' from the eastern hill ranges of the Democratic Republic of Congo, we have created a delicious, award-winning tonic water. Designed to enhance the very best gins, vodkas and fortified wines, like vermouth, fino sherry and white port.

REFRESHINGLY LIGHT INDIAN TONIC WATER

We use naturally occurring fruit sugars to develop our lighter tonic water. The blending of subtle botanical flavours with spring water and highest-quality quinine gives it the distinctively clean, crisp character of Indian Tonic Water, but with 46% fewer calories.

MEDITERRANEAN TONIC WATER

By blending the essential oils from the flowers, fruits and herbs that we have gathered from around the Mediterranean shores with highest-quality quinine from the 'fever trees' of the Democratic Republic of the Congo, we have created a delicate, floral tonic water.

REFRESHINGLY LIGHT MEDITERRANEAN TONIC WATER

With 46% fewer calories than our regular Mediterranean Tonic Water, we use fruit sugars to develop our lighter tonic water, meaning its delicious and low in calories. Contains natural flavours and no artificial sweeteners.

ELDERFLOWER TONIC WATER

By blending the essential oils from handpicked English elderflowers with quinine of the highest quality from the 'fever trees' of the Democratic Republic of the Congo, we have created a delicious, floral variation of our Indian tonic water.

AROMATIC TONIC WATER

By blending the gentle bitterness of South American angostura bark with aromatic botanicals, such as cardamom, pimento berry and ginger, we've created a delicious, unique tonic water that can be enjoyed with gin to make a Pink G&T or as a sophisticated soft drink on its own.

LEMON TONIC WATER

By blending the finest Sicilian lemons with spring water and quinine of the highest quality from the fever trees of the Democratic Republic of the Congo, we have created a delicious lemon tonic water with an authentic refreshing taste and aroma.

REFRESHINGLY LIGHT CUCUMBER TONIC WATER

Offering a delicate and fresh flavour, the light, crisp notes of cucumber essence are perfectly balanced with the gentle bitterness of our signature quinine from the fever trees of Eastern Congo. Blended with fruit sugar for 32% fewer calories than Fever-Tree Indian Tonic Water. The result is a tonic with an authentic and refreshing taste and aroma.

GINGERS

GINGER BEER

By brewing a blend of three gingers from Nigeria, Cochin and the Ivory Coast, we have created an award-winning ginger beer that has been highly acclaimed by gastronomes and critics alike. Not too sweet on the palate and with a deep, long-lasting ginger character. Perfect in a Dark & Stormy, Moscow Mule or simply as a soft drink on its own.

GINGER ALE

By using a unique blend of three of the world's finest naturally sourced gingers, subtle botanical flavours and spring water, we have created a delicious Ginger Ale with an authentic and refreshing taste and aroma. Perfectly balanced to enhance the flavour notes of the finest whiskies, bourbons and rums.

SMOKY GINGER ALE

We have combined our signature blend of three varieties of ginger with smoked applewood and subtle citrus to create a unique mixer that has been designed to enhance the finest whiskies and bourbons

SPICED ORANGE GINGER ALE

A unique blend of our signature gingers, combined with sweet clementine's and spicy cinnamon. The combination of ginger, citrus and spice has been crafted to complement the rich, full-bodied flavours found in the finest dark spirits, in particular cognacs & rums.

SODAS

PREMIUM SODA WATER

By using soft spring water, bicarbonate of soda and a high level of carbonation, we've have created a delicious soda water with a delicate aroma. Perfect for bringing out the best flavours of the finest whiskies.

PINK GRAPEFRUIT SODA

Made with real juice from handpicked pink Florida grapefruits. An impressive upfront burst of fresh grapefruit carefully balanced with soft pink grapefruit floral notes. The perfect levels of carbonation and real juice content provide a rounded base which complements the best premium tequilas and vodkas for a refreshing, light spritz.

ITALIAN BLOOD ORANGE SODA

Juicy blood oranges from Sicily meet an iconic herbal blend to create our Italian Blood Orange Soda. This complex and sophisticated mixer pairs perfectly with premium vodka and Italian liqueurs.

LIME AND YUZU SODA

Our Lime and Yuzu Soda is made with Tahiti lime from Mexico's fertile groves in addition to pressed oil extract from the wonderfully floral Japanese yuzu to create a low-calorie soda that's perfect for mixing with premium vodka or tequila for a mouth-wateringly zesty summer spritz.

— DISTILLERY —
DIRECTORY

1919 DISTILLING, AUCKLAND

Nestled in the bustling industrial area of East Tamaki, 1919 Distilling prides itself on sourcing everything locally, even down to their custom made still, so that they can ensure the best quality and craftsmanship. Named for the year that New Zealand voted down prohibition they also stay true to the way gin was made in the 1900's by using ethanol made from sugar cane.

WEBSITE: 1919distilling.com

ADDRESS: Unit 17/375 East Tamaki Road, East Tamaki, Auckland

VISIT THEM: Distillery tours and tastings available by appointment

ARIKI SPIRIT, MOUNT MAUNGANUI

Tucked away in the balmy Bay of Plenty, Ariki Spirit crafts their gin using unique botanicals to achieve distinctive aromatic notes. Ariki means 'high chief' or 'leader' in Te Reo, with cognates throughout the Pacific, and is associated with carrying great prestige or mana, reflecting their ambition of bringing the 'Spirit of the Pacific' to the world.

WEBSITE: arikispirit.com

ARROWTOWN DISTILLERY, ARROWTOWN

Resting beneath the picturesque Coronet Peak, Arrowtown Distillery make small batches of handcrafted gin using pure artesian water. Started by two kiwi builders with a fondness for gin and an eye for sustainability, they use a selection of botanicals from the local area much like the foraging of the namesakes of their gin for nuggets during the gold rush.

WEBSITE: riftersgin.com

BATCH10 SPIRITS, PUHOI

Located in the idyllic backwoods of Puhoi, batch10 Spirits was started by a bunch of mates in one of their sheds infusing premium bourbon with local native bush honey. Having grown and developed since then they now make a range of distilled spirits crafted from the finest New Zealand and international ingredients.

WEBSITE: batch10.com

BEGIN DISTILLING, NEW PLYMOUTH

Situated in New Plymouth's suburb of Westown near the start of Surf Highway 45, Begin Distilling is the home of Juno Gin. Following their three key values of "Make it Fun", "Make it Together", and "Make it Right" they engage with horticulturalists and researchers to locally source botanicals, and show their efficacy and flavour potential. They are also working with Massey University to create a world-first juniper plantation in New Zealand.

WEBSITE: junogin.com

ADDRESS: 16 Sunley Street, Westown, New Plymouth

VISIT THEM: Distillery tours and tastings available by appointment

BLACK COLLAR DISTILLERY, KERIKERI

Situated near Kerikeri in the tranquil Bay of Islands, the beating heart of Black Collar is their gorgeous handmade copper pot still called 'Frankie'. Completely old school with no automation or computer programs, it's all down to the knowledge and fine tuning of the distiller to capture just the right qualities to produce their gin.

WEBSITE: blackcollardistillery.com

BROKEN HEART SPIRITS, ARROW JUNCTION

Nestled in the foothills of the Southern Alps near picturesque Arrowtown, Broken Heart Spirits was born from the memory of a beloved life lost. They endeavour to create gin that captures the glory days of a friendship between two Germans that met in the South Island and bonded over their mutual appreciation for creating fine spirits before one of them tragically passed away.

WEBSITE: brokenheartspirits.com

ADDRESS: 1 Powder Terrace, Arthurs Point, Queenstown

VISIT THEM: Gin Garden open daily

BUREAUCRATS GIN LTD., WELLINGTON

Located in the windy capital city of Wellington, Bureaucrats Gin Ltd. was started by two bureaucrats with the hobby of distilling gin in their home laundries. Driven by a love of fine gin and fine things, they used the age old method of trial and error until they had developed a distillation consistency and quality which they could share with the world. Producing small batches, they focus on innovation and bold botanical combinations.

WEBSITE: bureaucratsgin.co.nz

CARBONSIX DISTILLERY, AUCKLAND

Embedded in the bustling heart of Takapuna on Auckland's North Shore, CarbonSix Distillery like to make things that are unique and different. Producing a wide range of small batch spirits, their gin collection focuses on creating diverse flavours, using various fruits and botanicals, with natural colours from the maceration process.

WEBSITE: carbonsix.co.nz
ADDRESS: 16B Como Street, Takapuna, Auckland
VISIT THEM: Tasting room open daily

THE CARDRONA DISTILLERY, CARDRONA

Tucked up in the breath-taking Cardrona Valley between Wanaka and Queenstown, The Source Gin is produced on-site at The Cardrona Distillery. They use a single malt spirit in their two bespoke, handmade copper pot stills all the way from Scotland and abstain from chill-filtering in order to achieve a fuller flavour and character.

WEBSITE: cardronadistillery.com
ADDRESS: 2125 Cardrona Valley Road, Wanaka, Otago
VISIT THEM: Cellar Door open daily, distillery tours available by appointment.

CONCEPT BESPOKE DISTILLING, CHRISTCHURCH

Seated in the historic Sydenham suburb of Christchurch, Concept Brewing & Distilling are a micro craft brewery/ distillery using all natural ingredients with a 'support local' ethos at their core. As far as they're concerned, the closer to home it is the better it is, from local industry to local people and local suppliers.

WEBSITE: concept-brewing.myshopify.com

COROMANDEL DISTILLING CO., THAMES

Stationed in Thames just a stone's throw from the Coromandel Forest Park and the Kauaeranga Valley where they source their water and several botanicals, Coromandel Distilling Co. produce boutique gins using a custom 150L, German-made Carl still. As members of the 1% for the Planet organisation they give 1% of their revenue to conservation to preserve the wilderness that they benefit from.

WEBSITE: corodc.com

ADDRESS: 'The Depot' 715 Pollen Street, Thames, Coromandel Penisula

VISIT THEM: Distillery open Friday - Saturday.

**DANCING SANDS
DISTILLERY**

DANCING SANDS DISTILLERY, TAKAKA

Bundled away in the small town of Takaka in the Tasman region's beautiful Golden Bay area, Dancing Sands Distillery sources their water from the aquifer that feeds the nearby Te Waikoropupu Springs, often regarded as the clearest spring water in the world. They make all of their gins in small 150 litre batches to allow for maximum control over quality without any automation, instead using taste, temperature, and touch to achieve their results.

WEBSITE: dancingsands.com

ADDRESS: 46A Commercial Street, Takaka, Nelson Tasman

VISIT THEM: Cellar door open Monday - Saturday

DENZIEN URBAN DISTILLERY, WELLINGTON

Standing in the heart of Wellington's vibrant central Te Aro suburb, Denzien Urban Distillery is an artisan gin distillery with a mission to make brazen city gins for city people. They produce small batches in their handmade copper pot still and use distilled rainwater, all of which can be watched in person before tasting at their visitable location.

WEBSITE: denzien.nz

ADDRESS: 10 Lombard Street, Te Aro, Wellington

VISIT THEM: Cellar door open Tuesday to Sunday

DISTILLERIE DEINLEIN, TE PUNA

Sequestered away between the Kaimai Ranges and Tauranga, Distillerie Deinlein uses a copper reflux still operated by a master distiller that can trace their distilling heritage back 90 years to Germany. Their gin is inspired by and named for the very rare and endangered Chatham Island's Black Robin, and they donate to Forest & Bird for every bottle sold to help protect NZ's native wildlife for future generations.

WEBSITE: distillerie.co.nz

ECOLOGY & CO., AUCKLAND

Set amongst the industry and commerce of Wairau Valley on Auckland's North Shore, Ecology & Co. are a social enterprise and artisanal distiller that produces alcohol-free spirits. They strive to make flavourful and aromatic drinks that give the same fulfilling experience as other alcohol-filled favourites but are sugar-free, carb-free, fat-free, and alcohol free.

WEBSITE: ecologyandco.com

ELEMENTAL DISTILLERS, BLENHEIM

Stationed out in the fertile Wairau Plain at the heart of the Marlborough wine region, Elemental Distillers create small batches using a boutique 200 litre copper pot still and a sustainable neutral base spirit. They work closely with independent farmers, foragers, and cooperative to ensure that they get the finest quality botanicals from those who know and grow them best while striving for complete transparency, going from root to cup.

WEBSITE: elementaldistillers.com

ADDRESS: 195 Rapaura Road, Rapaura, Blenheim

VISIT THEM: Distillery tours and tastings available by appointment.

FENTON STREET DISTILLERY, STRATFORD

Huddled beneath the slopes of Mt Taranaki in the town of Stratford which is full of Shakespearian references, like many of their gins, Fenton Street Distillery has grown out of its founders' restoration of their 1920s neo-classical building. They are one of the smallest commercial distilleries in New Zealand, making deliberately small 48 litre batches to achieve a genuinely handcrafted product.

WEBSITE: fentonartscollective.co.nz/distillery

ADDRESS: 11 Fenton Street, Stratford

VISIT THEM: Tastings available by appointment

GOOD GEORGE DISTILLERY, HAMILTON

Cloistered in the industrial suburb of Frankton in Hamilton, Good George Distillery resides in the former St George's Church from which they take their name. Originally started as a brewery, they also began making hand sanitiser in early 2020 as part of Operation Helping Hands and later decided to give their stills a day off from that project and make some gin too.

WEBSITE: goodgeorge.kiwi.nz

GREY LYNN GIN, AUCKLAND

Nestled in the charming central Auckland suburb of Grey Lynn, Grey Lynn Gin was conceived during the rising of the sun one New Year's Day in the pursuit of a bold gin that stands out when mixed. Handcrafted in a small garage, all of their distillation, bottling, and labelling is done by hand.

WEBSITE: greylynngin.com

HASTINGS DISTILLERS, HASTINGS

Situated near the edge of central Hastings in the fertile alluvial Heretaunga Plains, Hastings Distillers was New Zealand's first organic certified producer of spirits and liqueurs. They endeavour to grow as many of their botanicals as possible in the Hawke's Bay using organic and biodynamic practices, with the belief that the region's 'terroir' imprints on all of the botanicals. Once distilled they cut to strength using spring water from the nearby Kaweka Ranges.

WEBSITE: hastingsdistillers.com

ADDRESS: 231 Heretaunga Street East, Hastings

VISIT THEM: Cellar door open Wednesday to Saturday

HERRICK CREEK DISTILLERY, CHRISTCHURCH

Positioned in the idyllic beachside suburb of New Brighton in Christchurch, Herrick Creek is a nano-distillery making a variety of spirits in small batches using local ingredients. They take their name and inspiration from the legend of the South Island Moose with the goal of providing unique spirits influenced by North American creators.

WEBSITE: herrickcreek.co.nz

HUMDINGER GIN, GERALDINE

Surrounded by the tapestry of the Canterbury Plains in Geraldine, Humdinger Gin take pride in the history of their building, the 'old Morrison's Garage', and still with a 50L copper pot and 3-plate column. They focus on natural products that are truly recognisable in nature and a respect for the bees that make them all possible.

WEBSITE: humdinger.nz
ADDRESS: 3a Talbot Street, Geraldine
VISIT THEM: Open daily for tastings and informal tours when time allows.

IMAGINATION, REIKORANGI

Sheltered in the lush foothills of the Reikorangi Valley on the Kapiti Coast, imagination is housed on the original site of the pioneering Tuatara Beer Brewery which they use to draw inspiration from. They produce small batch seasonal gins using a copper plate fractionating column still and pure rainwater captured on the property, and source many of their ingredients locally from family owned operations and backyard gardeners.

WEBSITE: imaginationgin.nz

ISLAND GIN DISTILLERY, GREAT BARRIER ISLAND

Secreted away on the remote but beautiful Great Barrier Island, Island Gin Distillery has a sustainable ethos towards producing their small batch gins. Their bottles are designed to reflect a Kina shell and are made with almost 50% reclaimed glass, meaning that just like no two kina shells are alike, neither are their bottles. All of their gins are distilled in small batches using a copper still before heading to their solar-powered bottling line.

WEBSITE: islandgin.com

KAIMAI BREWING AND DISTILLING CO., WAIKINO

Based at the historic Waikino Hotel in the Coromandel's beautiful Karangahake Gorge, Kaimai Brewing and Distilling Co. hand craft single batch gins. Inspired by old stories of the gold mining era, they celebrate the heritage of the land as well as the people and history of the gorge and surrounding areas.

WEBSITE: kaimaibrewinganddistilling.co.nz

KINGS LIQUOR, AUCKLAND

Huddled on the northern edge of Auckland in the suburb of Rosedale, Kings Liquor has been making spirits since 1985. They produce small, handcrafted, artisanal batches of triple distilled gin which is echoed in their hand-illustrated labels that reflect the traditional crafting and blending of their recipes.

WEBSITE: kingsliquor.co.nz

KIWI SPIRITS DISTILLERY, MOTUPIPI

Sheltered in the beautiful Golden Bay area of the Tasman region, Championz are a world away from the hustle and bustle of city life. Focusing on small batch distillation to deliver superior quality, they are committed to attention to detail and using all-natural ingredients to produce the best preservative-free spirits. They endeavour to minimise their impact on the world by taking a sustainable approach to their craft.

WEBSITE: kiwispiritdistillery.co.nz
ADDRESS: 430 Abel Tasman Drive, Motupipi
VISIT THEM: Distillery and tasting room open daily.

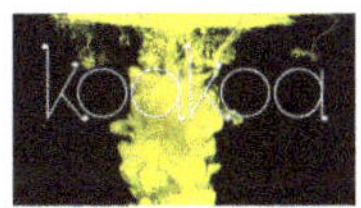

KOAKOA, PARAPARAUMU BEACH

Situated just a couple of minutes away from the Paraparaumu Beach shoreline on the spectacular Kapiti Coast, Koakoa which means 'happiness' in Te Reo) distil both liqueurs and spirits. They use sustainable New Zealand ingredients and water filtered down from the Tararua ranges to "make fine stuff, without the stuffiness", and "give people what they want".

WEBSITE: koakoa.nz
ADDRESS: 3c Magrath Avenue, Paraparaumu Beach
VISIT THEM: Tasting room open Monday - Friday.

LADY H SPIRITS, AUCKLAND

Conceived in a garage in the depths of Central Otago and fully realised in Auckland, Lady H Spirits was started with the drive of creating a gin that would make the best martini. They aim to show the world something a little different that can sing from its own song sheet.

WEBSITE: ladyhspirits.com

LAVENDER HILL, RIVERHEAD

Secluded on the outskirts of the historic township of Riverhead to the north of Auckland, Lavender Hill operates from a small working farm. Their central philosophy is to create products with a connection to the land and superb provenance, using handcrafted and sustainable ingredients to achieve this.

WEBSITE: lavenderhill.co.nz
ADDRESS: 11 Beacon Road, Riverhead, Auckland
VISIT THEM: Cellar door open by appointment.

LIGHTHOUSE GIN DISTILLERY, MARTINBOROUGH

Located in the warm micro-climate of Martinborough in the Wairarapa that supports a thriving local agriculture and viticulture, Lighthouse Distillery is one of New Zealand's oldest craft gin makers. Taking inspiration from the region's iconic Cape Palliser Lighthouse and its association with craftsmanship, they only use the purest water filtered from high in the nearby Remutaka Ranges in their twice distilled gins.

WEBSITE: lighthousegin.co.nz
ADDRESS: 89 Martins Road, Martinborough
VISIT THEM: Available to taste at the Te Kairanga Cellar Door

MT. FYFFE DISTILLERY, KAIKOURA

Arrayed amongst the foothills of Mount Fyffe near stunning Kaikoura, Mt. Fyffe Distillery forage many of their botanicals from around their own sheep farm on the slopes, and the local area. They use a Portuguese 40L copper alembic still to craft small batches with their own spring water which are bottled and labelled by hand.

WEBSITE: mtfyffedistillery.co.nz

GUIDE TO NEW ZEALAND GIN

NO8 DISTILLERY, DUNEDIN

Tucked into the Dog with Two Tails café & bar in the outer ring of Dunedin's Octagon, No8 Distillery take their name from the mentality and saying that arose from fixing anything with a piece of number 8 wire. This carries through into their experimental and unconventional approach to extraction and reconfigurable Franken-still named "Therese".

WEBSITE: no8distillery.com

ADDRESS: 25 Moray Place, Dunedin Central

VISIT THEM: Distillery and cellar door open Monday - Saturday

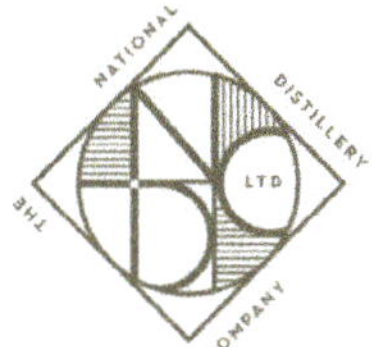

THE NATIONAL DISTILLERY CO., NAPIER

Ensconced in the commercial-industrial northern waterfront of Napier, The National Distillery Co. resides in one of the cities architectural crown jewels. Built in 1931 following the Napier earthquake, it reflects the influences of Art Nouveau and Modernism, or Art Deco, that were in vogue at the time. They blend modern distilling techniques with time-honoured traditions, looking to this duality to inspire their creativity and overall approach to gin making.

WEBSITE: nationaldistillery.nz

ADDRESS: 1 Ossian Street, Ahuriri

VISIT THEM:
Distillery open Thursday - Friday (extended seasonally)

PAPAKA ROAD DISTILLERY, NGUNGURU

Anchored on the northern bank of the Ngunguru River in the stunning Tutukaka Coast, Papaka Road Distillery aim to create product that is unique to their slice of Northland. They are focused on creating a signature taste using natural botanicals and fresh, locally sourced produce along with water from the pristine river catchment.

WEBSITE: papakaroad.co.nz

PINK & WHITE GEOTHERMAL GIN, ROTORUA

Surrounded by the geothermal wonders of Rotorua, Pink & White - Geothermal Gin take their name from the famed terraces that were lost in the 1886 eruption of Mount Tarawera and town's history of hospitality. Their vision is to build a distillery that utilises 100% renewable geothermal energy through a boiler to produce the most sustainable spirit.

WEBSITE: pinkandwhite.co.nz

PREMIUM LIQUOR CO., AUCKLAND

Set amongst the sprawl and variety of Auckland city, Premium Liquor Co. produce a wide range of products. They hand craft and triple distil their Rose & Twig gins in small batches, each with five different botanicals, to make each one unique and emphasise the beauty in being different.

WEBSITE: premiumliquor.co.nz

REEFTON DISTILLING CO., REEFTON

Stationed deep in the Inangahua River Valley in the West Coast town of Reefton, Reefton Distilling Co.'s gin, Little Biddy, is named in honour of the local legend Bridget 'Biddy' Goodwin, a pipe-smoking, gin-toting, 4-foot-tall gold prospector who lived in the 1800s. A modern distillery in an age-old town, they use large numbers of native botanicals from the surrounding rainforest to achieve a distinct West Coast flavour.

WEBSITE: reeftondistillingco.com
ADDRESS: 10 Smith Street, Reefton
VISIT THEM: Distillery and cellar door open daily

REID + REID DISTILLERY, MARTINBOROUGH

Based in the warm micro-climate of Martinborough in the Wairarapa that supports a thriving local agriculture and viticulture, Reid + Reid Distillery was founded in 2015 by two brothers with backgrounds in engineering and beverage production. They seek to challenge the perception of a 'classic' gin and promote New Zealand's unique native flora.

WEBSITE: reidandreid.co.nz
ADDRESS: 145 Todds Road, Martinborough
VISIT THEM: Tasting room open Saturdays over summer months

RIOT & ROSE SPIRITS LTD., BLENHEIM

Established in Blenheim at the heart of the Marlborough wine region, Riot & Rose is one of only a handful of distilleries in New Zealand that are female owned and operated. Forefronting this in their brand and ethos, they aim to create contemporary gins that allow you to reflect your own style. This is emphasised by the way that their gins are based on different time periods which were poignant in gin history.

WEBSITE: riotandrose.com

RUIN DISTILLERY, MOONSHINE VALLEY

Perched on the side of the quiet Moonshine Valley next to Upper Hutt, Ruin Distillery takes its name from the old gin moniker 'mother's ruin' in a wry nod and as a challenge to rise up. Possibly one of the world's smallest commercial distilleries at only 4m2, they combine 30 years of home distilling experience and a six plate flute still to produce small batches in individually numbered bottles.

WEBSITE: ruindistillery.co.nz

SANDYMOUNT DISTILLERY, OTAGO PENISULA

Cloaked by the hills of the Otago Peninsula beneath Pukehiki and Larnach Castle, Sandymount Distillery is fed by spring water from below their farm and surrounded by abundant native flora. They take inspiration from the beautiful landscape around them and its history in creating their handcrafted, small batches.

WEBSITE: sandymount.nz

SCAPEGRACE DISTILLING CO., CHRISTCHURCH

Tucked away in the 'Garden City' of Christchurch, Scapegrace Distilling Co. makes their gin using glacial water that takes 80 years to filter through the rock of the Southern Alps before being released into an aquifer. They use a restored 19th century hand-beaten copper pot still to create their gins in the same way it was done back then. This is reflected in their bottles which are a modern take on the genever (Dutch gin) bottles from 200 years ago.

WEBSITE: scapegracedistillery.com

THE SPIRITS WORKSHOP DISTILLERY, CHRISTCHURCH

Established in the light industrial area of Christchurch's suburb Sydenham, Curiosity Gin set out from their start to create truly unique and individual gins that stand out from the crowd. To hold true to these values their gins are made "grain to glass" where possible, in small batches using their copper pot still.

WEBSITE: thespiritsworkshop.co.nz

ADDRESS: 11 Sandyford Street, Sydenham

VISIT THEM: Distillery tours available via appointment, cellar door open Monday – Saturday.

THOMSON WHISKY DISTILLERY, RIVERHEAD

Based in the historic township of Riverhead to the north of Auckland, Victor Gin was born out of tinkering and experimentation at the Thomson Whisky Distillery. Taking inspiration from the world of music they focus on fresh botanicals and the heavy use of juniper to create the best spirits they can.

WEBSITE: thomsonwhisky.com

TWELFTH HOUR DISTILLERY, AUCKLAND

Ringed by the vibrant communities of South Auckland, Twelfth Hour was born from a small group of friends' desire to fuse fresh, exotic botanicals from around the globe with New Zealand made gin. They hand craft small batches, spending many nights working well past midnight, which is the origin of their name.

WEBSITE: twelfthhourdistillery.co.nz

THE VICARS SON, AUCKLAND

Produced in the heart of Point Chevalier in Auckland with a zero waste policy, The Vicar's Son is the smallest commercial distillery in the world. Operating a 6L finishing still that produces a max of nine bottles per batch, they don't use any filtering techniques so that what you see and taste is as it came out of the still.

WEBSITE: vicarsson.co.nz

WAIHEKE DISTILLING CO., WAIHEKE

Enveloped by bush and former pasture land on the eastern end of Waiheke Island, Waiheke Distilling Co. have developed a large garden that exemplifies the botanical story of their spirits. Overlooking Cowes Bay, with its history of hospitality and leisure, they focus on crafting botanical spirits in a sustainable and meaningful way.

WEBSITE: waihekedistilling.co.nz

ADDRESS: 258 Cowes Bay Road, Waiheke Island

VISIT THEM: Cellar door open via appointment, closed during winter months

WASHHOUSE DISTILLERY, WAITOKI

Secluded amongst the many dairy farms that surround the small town of Waitoki to the north of Auckland, Washhouse Distillery makes small batches in a handmade copper alembic still from Portugal in what was once a home garage. They pride themselves on the manual nature of their process and lack of pretence.

WEBSITE: washhousedistillery.co.nz

WILD DIAMOND DISTILLERY, QUEENSTOWN

Resting on the Kelvin Peninsula overlooking Lake Wakatipu and Queenstown, Wild Diamond takes its name from the natural elements that surround them. They select their botanicals based on their quality and character, sourcing them both internationally and locally. Maintaining their connection to their environment, their stills are powered by renewable wind and water energy, and invest back into water and aquatic habitat enhancement, recovery, and restoration.

WEBSITE: wilddiamond.co.nz

THE WHITE SHEEP CO., WHANGAMATA

Located in the popular beach town of Whangamata which borders The Coromandel Forest Park, The White Sheep Co. is a boutique distillery that handcrafts a range of spirits and liqueurs using premium New Zealand sheep's milk. The milk takes two weeks to ferment using special yeasts and is then distilled into a full strength spirit using a traditional style copper still to retain some of the sheep milk's flavours.

WEBSITE: thewhitesheepco.com

www.ingramcontent.com/pod-product-compliance
Lightning Source LLC
Chambersburg PA
CBHW050027040726
47599CB00015B/1566